The boy in the purple room

The Boy in the Purple Room

by

David Axtell

Published by David Axtell
in association with Studio 7 Arts

Studi● 7
E
V
E
N

Printed and bound by
Clays Ltd, Suffolk

A CIP catalogue of this book is available from
the British Library

ISBN 978-1-5272-2429-2

In memory of Ben Dorling
and our worthy warriors

Oxford forever and a day

The Boy In The Purple Room
by
David Axtell

Contents

Only the beginning
(aka Dirty Time Co.)

"Try it, you'll like it"
Agnew on your wrist
Caper in Osaka
Progress and harmony dissolving
As priest tries to kill Pope Paul VI
Yuppies invade Manson trial
Cease and desist theme recalled
On quadraphonic player
That might be deadly or
Becomes all the rage
Knife wielding readers
Run on commercials
Losing marbles in soup
Sponsoring Adidas All-Stars
High on your list
Flares and foliant sideburns
A must see Convoy
Free Wheelin' Fritz the Cat
In the Hat
Imagine Easy Rider on a Chopper
In black and white
More than ever now
Dress around in average seconds
Take a Polaroid of a boat neck shirt
Listen to music you can't dance to
Go to bed early
After all
"The eighties are gonna be something wonderfully
new and different."

OX3

Carve your name on the city walls
and walk hand in hand
through gaps of learned streets
what joys to meet in summer fairs
gallopers of St. Giles' feast
amidst bustling rose madder stalls

Down in Albion's golden heirs
laid out from Lent in oft busy wares
sown sunshine will wash our feet
warm summer climes drift on by
dried out rains blown on high
as dreaming spires chime eternal sleep

Guilty pleasures driven home
by boys dressed in white
make up the dawn
let's mow the lawn
and sing Jerusalem
in this new morn light

Where the childermass roam and wander still
alongside regicides unable to atone encaenia's rule
bystanders hunting the snark break into song
with Aristotle and Giotto baying for contention
for the Queen of Hearts *(if truth be told)*
of tender love denied

Bequeathed atop Comprigney hill
and laid to rest beneath the Tyburn Tree
where the gallows roost resides
and where the sweetest kisses
fell from the crows
were dealt a hefty blow
on all old England's wounds

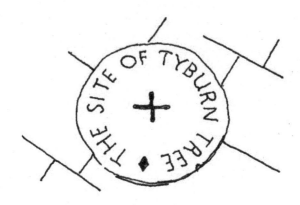

The Turf

Bell hopping on my way to The Turf
Swaying under the Bridge of Sighs
Everyone had Blackbird eyes but me
I took another swig at the bar and then I let slip
My pocket full of rye

"It's no gold of mine" I said
Having a nose for trouble this time
I lit an explosive cigar for my next of kin
Like a lead balloon I slunk to the floor

Underneath the table real ale in hand
Learning the crux of the matter
Despite my best intentions never to lie
I always found the answer to the crime
More palatable when baked in a pie

Castle Mound

REX ERIT QUI RECTE FACIET
QUI NON FACIET, NON ERIT

13 balls

Gilbert, white, harry, boat
watery molly, william, parry
freeman, rothe, walter jeoffrey
dunn, green and boulton

went to mow a meadow

Rollright Stones

Losing count of the Rollright Stones
won't somebody pinch me
tell me I'm not dreaming
you made an atom bomb
under the stairs
paralytic memories
will sap you
black dog seasons
will engulf you
and blow you away
like lions for lambs
set them free
don't blame me or
the whispering knights
plotting treason
it's got nothing to do with us

Warneford Flowers

Isn't it a pity losing your mind in the city
lost daydreams and butterflies
amongst the Warneford flowers

It's been a long, long time coming
descending 20,000 miles an hour
got to slow right down

Waking up with your head in the clouds
who's watching the red hand gang?
someone whispered 'peace'
here comes the moon man
can you hear him crying?

Isn't it a pity losing your mind to the city
lost daydreams and butterflies
amongst the Warneford flowers
where we talked for hours and hours

A mind that just might break
someone whispered 'peace'
here comes the moon man
can you hear him trying?

Hinksey Hill

Climbing above Hinksey Hill
Overseeing William Golding's Spire
Wedding belles sing out a Midsummer's ball
A tug of war ensues across Folly Bridge
Beating the bounds on convention hounds
Baying for blood and a put upon career
Old Tom's hanging by a wire
Such a pretty postcard of a town

The gown can see their futures paved in gold
A cut above the rest just passing through
Bequeathed by birds carrying feather voices
They walk tall but they make you feel small
Become a defender of the town
I'm not going to have my dreams burnt down

You have to watch what you say
They'll burn you at the stake on Broad Street
Tell all ye faithful what to think
Dressed in whites I know me rights
I'd rather give gode knocks at Swindlestock
Before gloating in battle at Swansdown

Why don't you bury me beneath Magdalen Bridge
With my head served on a platter
(The sixth former maybe not the latter)
You know you're never too young to lay down
Firm foundations on St. Scolastica Day
In such a pretty postcard of a town

birdman

Caged birds behind back garden barricades
were our flights of fancy

shoals of life unweaving the rainbow
keen to grasp seminole latitudes
oblivious to battles in the streets below

advancing dovecote messengers
apostles with shorn dustbin lids for protection
shielding threats from mars

pursuers shaking off war torn tinder sticks
found yomping over lye valley and fairview
oblivious to the deaf and dumb birdman

whose body work to body work co-existence
kept our distant sheltered lives
wholesome for generations to come

until modern archaeologists
those keen forensic saboteurs
exploited and cajoled by simmering home brews

let the cat out of the bag
scattering lead lined coffins
that once threatened to defend our realm

and those who lost King Alfred's jewel
looked upon our graven skies
in heavens true unveiling

to the sage upon the stage
as we replayed Higgs boson again

The Price

I lost myself near St. Sepluchre's fields
Mislaid circumstances you can never see
Only to hear
The thunderclap of April showers
Come bearing down on me

Someday I'll bring you flowers
But I've got a heart of stone and
I feel waylaid by a state of play
When life's mapped out so differently

A View from the Bridge trying to fit in
But it gets so dark
Waiting by the coaching stones
And then I have to go in

Maybe by tomorrow on the new morn tide
Where the banks change their name
I'll keep a hold on giving
And I won't feel afraid to try

Cast through the sails
Of The Fighting Temeraire
I look upon your golden rays and I can see
Nodding doubts of love I fear
Something that I'm not quite ready for

Someday I'll bring you flowers
But I've got a heart of stone and
I feel waylaid by a state of play
When life's mapped out so very differently

A View from the Bridge trying to fit in
But it gets so dark
By maybe tomorrow
I won't feel afraid to try

The Slade

Timepieces entombed in glass on the mantle shelf
Tells no time at all
The Bullseye competitors scored at seven
As Powder Monkeys plying with touch paper pictures
Congregate on the floor
Two courses away from Cherwell and Evenlode
Un-bottled when rainbows touched the ground
Brings home the morning
Ermine White Horses asleep on the hillsides share visions
Of Michelangelo where vaulted ceilings of Eden once stood
And off peak dial tones sheltered from the era of St. Francis
Tells no tale at all

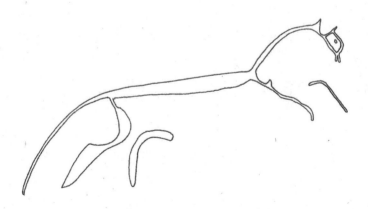

Pathways

Barking like a dog, smelling like a cat
Water rats hiding inside tin cans
Weave fibre optic spaghetti junctions
Plundering our neon soul centre functions whole

Blackened tar bleeds across ferry link fields
Carving through bituminous greenbelt sights
Etched and embedded upon a saxon crossways
Carfax steel gauge tramway ripped up

Only going as far as the Plain
Dring's excursions cantered on until hidden electronics
Of the mid 1960's became retracted opportunities
Going nowhere near the Old Road heights

'Titup-Titup' passing by in all but name
A thoroughfare towards The World's End
To make headway for a century and a half
Of colonial monopolies trading on their spoils

Lutyens' Indian Gate ready made to circumvent
An empires peril from the burning of Rheims
A future partition torn free to roam among Spitalfields
Nescient day levels of Roman excavations in the rains

Hung drawn and quartered the disinterred spew
Customised to flit upon Blake's Westminster Abbey view
Before our ancestors burial realms were put on the shelf
A diocese laying to rest the last vendetta of gin house wealth

Conjuring tumultuous crowds on the Underground
Feeding a frenzy to catch the last train from Euston
Queuing for a flight of fancy from Heathrow to Houston
Breaking the sound barrier four hours later on launchpad two

Building sky high bridges to the Karman line
A Twentieth Century gateway
The new sixty mile high expressway
Stolen from little boy blue

Galileo mankind has reached a feat of epic proportions
Not least from the ascendency of Copernicus sky prophets
Zero-X trail blazers crowd funding re-usable rockets,
Space Station Dragon crew docks and Rosetta rocks

For a new beat hapenin' to Mars...

King of the Spires

In the bath at the bar
The man with the painted face
Was looking kind of sad
At all those fools
Selling big issues in the rain

Drinking too much so I can feel better
The river Isis never tasted so good
King of the Spires
Light the fires
Wash away and float free

You know you should take another sip
When the singing butler passes you by
Taking a stroll across the Plain
Between Towns Road
Where I held up my mind
Two girls playing chess in The Cape
Were calling out another day

King of the Spires
Light the fires
Burn away the night with me

As the leaves fall and
The days hold their sway
I'll be calling out your refrain
Late again walking on the borderline
Trying to keep afloat in the rain
Watching the head teacher leaving
Reminded me of the games
When we play away

It's cold and dark
But I'm happy on Morrell Avenue
I need to soak away these feelings
Because it fires me out-in

A lifetime's ambition
Calling out for your refrain
King of the Spires
Wash away and float free
Light the fires
King of the Spires
Light the fires and
Burn away the night

Wash away and float free
Wash away and float free

With me

Iron Sycamore

Sure. I feel fine today in Bonn Square
But is this peace really the same
In the year eighteen hundred and seventy three?

Would I still carry a flame for you?

They felled our tree a long time ago
No bough to sit on or cradle to rock
No questions asked of the silent witness
St. Peter le Bailey
Demolished in the dock

Will I miss you ever after?
When we traversed a route over the Kyber Pass...

Misbelieving my eyes
Blue wrapped bodies
Unearthed beside the Tirah memorial
For want of a preservation order
Sent to cut you down
In your prime

After our troops stormed Dargai Heights
Run-of-the-river now gives power to those sights

Sure. I feel fine at Bonn Square today
But is this the same war
In the year two thousand and eight?
When they find out

I dug up your roots

Britpop Alcools

It's back in the black to the new Sensation
Grooving at the river in my Sound City
New Labours Piltdown Man lives in No.10
When Giddens South Sea Bubble reinvented Hubble!
The Third Way was all the rage in this day and age
(Forty five minutes later we'd soon all be in trouble)

Neither OK Computer or Hale Bop was a flop
When Hong Kong got given the chop
The Karma Police were all over the shop
With Theakston, Ball and a happy birthday swap
At the present Astoria

On the cover of this month's Face
Titanic Ashcroft has a bitter sweet fax just for you
'Study fruitful ever last, moth like to a burnt out candle wick'

Marking up De la Rue bills required great skill
To deposit within the newly independent Bank of England
A lifetime's worth of rave pills that couldn't save John Denver

Until Shoegazing quit your Fender style at V Festival
Rating Star Wars special editions missing a trick
On a Thrust SCC with Alan Partridge
Shooting Stars for a headline on TFI Friday
Framing Emin's Turner Prize outburst live on TV

Grosse Pointe Blank in ready-to-wear Alexander McQueen
Austin Powers swapping Dolly's clones with Swampy
Bronze Fruits filed under Harry Potter's Gold Smarties Prize
Half-baked in a Lost World of Monserrat ash
Pathfinder landing a Sojourner of truth on Independence Day
Retrieved from dead paparazzi on a French underpass

Tellin' Stories with Steve Lamacq
Katrina and the waves shining a light at last
One to one Kate Moss acting boss in Kowalski
On tour selling HIStory down the Thames
In it for the money. At the end of the day
Ladies and gentlemen we are floating in space

D'You Know What I Mean?
Only you.
You Beetlebum

As is now by the pool side in August
Be Here Now spelled the year 1997 out
Which somehow magically passed through you

Talk of the town

From the Tower of the Winds
Casting over seven pillars beyond Observatory Street
Our Delphi Oracle rests upon a pedestal
Bathed in Pythia's celestial light
Broadcasting her Music of the Spheres

Transmitting gravitational waves
Conveying the city with her infinite prose
St. Frideswide blessed on High
Will surely illuminate
All Souls

Double Yellow

Pandas   between   ranks
     scuttle   taxi
Diesel   jostle   position
    shuttles   into

Alongside Orwellian siren suits
Displacing despondency on the streets
By emerging disco beats and Hunky Dory

Bloodied fists clench toward a two tone heavy
Curbing slightly,
averting a chicken curry takeaway

Bamboo curtains open on blistering lips of swing divas
Press one for the road
Press two,
       stairs
           unfolding
Going d
    o
     w
      n

Down on an even keel...s...l...o...w...l...y

Dropping a swagger,
swapping Yale keys in oyster shells
When the batteries are low hold her steady
Take back the night,
this day belongs to the prowlers

Treading on knifeboards back to back,
unyielding...not moving
Bi-Polar bears await the patient shoals of Buck's Fizz charms
Keeping warm on a double yellow shift of hemline
While onlookers escape in a viviparous throng in the shallows

(This last line of inquiry suits everyone fine)

Forresters

The gardens grew so high
until they hid all the ashlar stele stones
the animal farm gathered to watch
ghosts at play in the chunkey yard

Lay lines were handpicked by churls
burhs earmarked for seasonal skirmishes
delaying the harvest for instant death
on marsh fields

The days had been so long and dark
reaping only their mothers weeping
leaving a salient landform at hill end
then I awoke and realised you weren't there

never mind, they built tower blocks anyway

Quarry Hollow

Saccy's pit was put out to pasture
He's been laid to rest
By the new beautification
Of The League of Nations
Quest for coltan and lithium

And we've never had it so good

Seated on freestone
Think Tanks and Quangos
Seamlessly burned down Windmill cottages
Raising the literary bar at The Kilns
Turned out Risinghurst facades
And advanced Barton prefab housing

Planting mobile forests that talk
Whilst CS Lewis and Tolkien met
In Uplands well-read fable
Marconi sawed the map off Table Head
As The Daily Mail headline read

Elvis, King of Rock, Dies at 42

No wonder the old soldier
Is raising hell at Old Joan's
Facing south all day
Built to last under Sutton Hoo
They bought and sold you
No matter what the caste

Beyond the Roman Way
Beyond the Horizon
Above the Thames valley
'Eye in the sky'
The bells of Holy Trinity still chime

The tinnitus of my years

First Contact

What a pleasant view
For such a cool brit fool
Doesn't take much to comprehend
Headington girls' school

Pull up a chair on a real fire
Patent children's dreams for a novel idea
Hand over land for a thousand pounds
And send it by first class mail

Pull a tooth, smile a grin
Shake a house, cause a din
Give to Oxfam and live in sin
Tune into the BBC and listen to radio Caroline

Exist on a stable diet
Of everything you've ever bought
Rob back a six hundred year old relic
Make everyone carry a bag for life
Just like Joseph Merrick

In life class
She made contact first
I studied her constantly
She always portrayed a lovely
Derriere

The Boy In The Purple Room

Fallen to the floor
A makeover duvet under down
Near the Tam Tam by the bedside
Where the Mariner kept time
Was an accident waiting to happen

For The Boy In The Purple Room

The four year-long partnership
Busied themselves on the hillside
Playing hopscotch with the Pergamon man
Who came in from the cold
He wanted to merge with an orange polypup
Paving the way in education

For The Boy In The Purple Room

Downstairs Aunt Betty was waiting patiently
With the Judge and the Juke Glass in the kitchen
To pour over decimalisation with Lazy Susan
Years before the winter of discontent
Had served its purpose well

For The Boy In The Purple Room

Hopping off the witches hat to Wood Farm
After his Grandfathers number fourteen
Lent a rest back simplicity to ease the modern strain of life
Of barber shop charades short back and sides
He was forever indebted to his ercol wife

For The Boy In The Purple Room

Here Come The Double Deckers!
Playing Jokari with Aunt Sally
Keeping mum at the start of a new decade
Picking out Lady Chatterley's Lover again
To digest The Ways of Love on a Parker Knoll sofa
Goldring Lenco played A Whiter Shade of Pale

For The Boy In The Purple Room

September's rain

Do you remember the people under the stairs?
Jim and Hilda who we thought with in the Cold War
While we drank lemonade in September's rain
Let's go down Southfield you said
Along Moonrise Road forever blue

I can still see us quail high in the bunker
Watching off the deck shootouts hone in on a view
Now that we've grown times have changed
But I don't mind those side-hill lies
What they said in the papers was untrue anyway

You know it was always up to you
As I'm waiting in play in the rain
All those times follow through
Know that we've flown I guess it's true

The meaning of it all was forever blue

It's never going to be on the same par
But that was then and this is now
Sometimes I swale from afar
As those times filter through

Summer rules fade away
On the meaning of it all
In September's rain

Music man

Here comes the Music man
Make way for his moves
As he shuffles his feet down our street
Emanating within Green River Records

Chalky strums his chords
Trying to look different
Because when the day breaks
The soul man's gonna wake up for you

Here comes the Music man
Through your stereo
Wearing shades after dark
Keeping cool in the light of day

It's not hard to seek him out
He only needs three minutes more
A vinyl collector for His Masters Voice
Just like Chalkies NME before

When the day breaks
He'll wake up with you
Sounding on your radio

The Music man looks no different than today
Striding along the banks of the Green River
He's still got such a lot to do
Making your dreams come true

Here comes the Music man
Here comes the Music man
Here comes the Music man

Colliding Circles

Colliding Circles in my head,
Thought I heard you scream
Looked out my window
The sun was shining and the birds were singing
But no one was in my tree

I took a leaf from a dead man's quarry
Whose words I'd consumed
Telling me what it was I couldn't say
And put them on hold for another day

Many miles have I travelled
To the same places where history unfolds
Many days have I lost
Still, I'm here counting the cost
Waiting for the bailiff to come

Who earns the money? Who stole the show?
Tomorrow never knows (you know)
Better get up, better get down
Standing out from in the cold

Now I find I don't sleep very well
And the pallor of my mind
Keeps me from feeling fine
Do we still have the time?
To show the way back home

Who said it was going to be easy?
Who said it was ever going to be?
Who earns the money? Who stole the show?
I can't afford not to know

Colliding Circles in my head,
Though I heard you scream
I looked out my window
The sun was shining and the birds were singing
But no one was in my tree

I washed my hair in the sink
Turned off the TV to think
I walked to school cos I'm no fool
I took my chances and they made me

But tomorrow never knows (you know)

Now I find I don't sleep very well
And the pallor of my mind
Keeps me from feeling fine
Do we still have the time?
To show the way back home

Better get up, better get down
Standing out from in the cold

Who said it was going to be easy?
Who said it was ever going to be?
Who earns the money? Who stole the show?
I can't afford not to know

Seven miles high I thought I heard you scream
Looked out my window down at the scene
The sun was shining and the birds were singing
Colliding Circles in my dream

'Colliding Circles' was mentioned as a lost song title by John Lennon for the Revolver LP in the early print editions of 'Revolution in the Head' by Ian Macdonald. (Published in 1994)

Included without realising that for a number of years the song title was in fact made up by Martin Lewis. (Humourist, writer, Radio host, Film Producer and instigator of The Other Policeman's Ball revue.)

A further Martin Lewis title 'Pink litmus shirt' is also mentioned in the book as a lost George Harrison song.

Subsequent re-prints have omitted both titles.

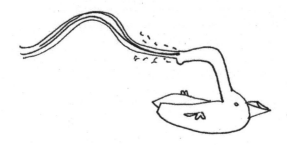

St. Francis

St. Francis helped us out for a while
when we pulled no punches

(we wore white Witney gloves)

Social gatherings became a sanctuary of sorts
solitarily appearances reflected on a black and white TV
fading away from the literary cordon that enclosed our minds
forbade us from delivering the bad news

(we surrendered the printers and sent them off to Hong Kong)

Our smoking guns hidden away in the hearthstone
wrapped in Early's four point blankets
became a reminder of those halcyon days
bobbies on the beat calling time
on set-aside weekly fixtures
consuming the torn up floorboards
revealing the one who had been laying all alone
waiting at platform two I knew you were guilty
she would never come home again

(we wished the giants marbles had landed on you)

Cromwell's shot gave a summer to remember
pretending never to have wept there alone
the schoolboys treasure in set one of the third year
worthy warriors, battle scarred every September
near the Slade roundabout
was a full stop. Gipsy lane turned into a headstone
ride and roses the new sound and united fans
exam schools our new abode for the next half dozen years
Not the Moulin Rouge and The Last Crusade a trilogy end

(we were content until they demolished The Manor ground,
The Six Bells & filled in our subway)

when we pulled no punches
St. Francis helped us out for a while

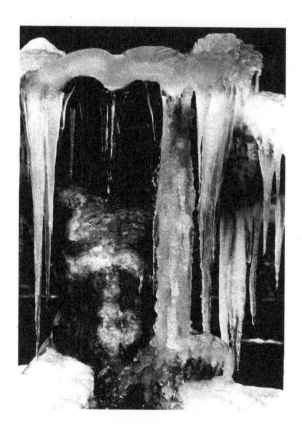

Little Cinnaminta smile!

Little Cinnaminta smile!
Summers here again
Won't you come out to play?
Little Cinnaminta
Summers here for you

There's no need to feel so low
See hear who goes where you go?
Little Cinnaminta smile!
Your Mother makes the flowers grow
Why don't you come out to play?

Gipsy eyes of emerald green
Where have you been?
How I've missed you
Up above everything seems so small
Feels like we're in a dream

Little Cinnaminta jumps the stile
Mile after mile
Pointing in turn every once in a while
When the moon is up as bright as day
Little Cinnaminta joins up the dots
Riding the Great Wain pinwheel in hand
Won't you come down today?

Little Cinnaminta smile!
Winters here
Won't you play in the snow?
Daddy said he built the moon for you
See hear who goes where you go?
Your Mother makes the flowers grow
Why won't you come out to play?

Little Cinnaminta smile!
Little Cinnaminta smile!
Just once in a while

Little Cinnaminta smile!
Little Cinnaminta smile!
Summers here again
Won't you come out to play?

Maid of all work

Living in a system
Working for no money
Young Lizzie
I'll always carry a flame for you

Set aside those fancy eyes
Swapping improvers
And dressing out shop walkers in pale blue
I'm up ready made for you

Come away from wrapping the houses
Let's step away from keen selling and
When the lights go out
I'll always carry a flame for you

This is Cape undressed
Seeking permission to sleep out with you
Young Lizzie what am I to do?
I'm falling head over heels
In love with you

The Ridgeway

At the 200 year celebrations of the Oxford Canal
I drew a picture of the event
I walked from Oxford to Banbury
And my legs were spent

Back in Jericho
The Phoenix played Another Month in the Country
Not My Own Private Idaho
I fell for Lucy and The Jennifers instead

Tears for Fears were my teenage peers
Jean-Michel Jarre's Oxygene part 4
Was the soundtrack to my young years

Raised on The Mary Rose, Grange Hill and Chocky
Blue Moon's Ms. Dipesto always took my calls
Detecting Tomorrow's World would morph online

Finding a bone handle in South Parks
Gave me an archaeological lean
Until the unexploded mortar shell blew apart that prize

Placing bets on the Common races
Near the Trout I never had a doubt
West Tip would win at Aintree

In extra time Howards End and Black Beauty
Gave me Absolute Conviction for Inspector Morse
Prisoner of Honour and $E=MC^2$ was par for the course
Fat Chance. Who Killed Harry Field?

Chemistry at the Delegacy got me as far as IC2
And our football league kept us all up to speed
Whoever wins buys a round at the next pub crawl

The Kings Arms or The Royal Oak?
The Eagle and Child another pint of mild
The Rose and Crown two more to down
The Lamb and Flag round three in the bag
Queue for the bar in the Chequers

Venue's too far. What's on at the Dolly?
Who? Carl Cox in Park End. It's ladies night!
'You can't come in Fifth Avenue not without a shirt mate.'
Are you kidding? Great now the girls have gone in

Let's step outside on the High
There's plenty of Kebab vans to soak up our sorrows
Let's get some cans. Wait. Sol's only a pound!
Ha ha, you are so wasted...feels like I'm on a boat
I think I'll float home instead

God I miss a night on the town

My Calamine

Sun drenched skin burnt to the bone
Lolling on a mat of my arm
Fingers dead on my face

A body map floating in space
Ready for touchdown

You've not had the last of it
My Calamine
Soothing follicles missing on bed springs
Covered head to toe in an ocean of lotion

Up to our necks in it
Putting us in our place
At Blodins pit
Sinking into a body of blue clay

My Calamine
Here marks the spot
Where I lost my first coat

Never to hang up again
On my old bed post

Guaifenesin

The wheeze of winter
Laid bare on your chest
Its machiavellian secretions
Plying inside damp lungs

Why not try the *'Anointed formulated medicine'*
To relieve chesty coughs
Hoarseness and sore throats

Possibly...

Helps loosen catarrh
That now keeps you awake

Apparently there are many varieties
To go through in one's lifetime

Ingredients change
Provided this 5ml medicine spoon
Is the correct opioid dose

Unsuitable only for those
Within range
Of ten years in age

PUMPKIN POLICE

Pumpkin Police
    Knocking at your door
By law are
    Warning shots
Programmed to invade
    Shoot down a child's cry
Your Privacy
    He was just holding a plastic toy
Your home
    Another failed raid
Your future is individually index-linked
    Still. All that's said and done
By Law
    Your family
Kept on file under lock and key. You
    Can be got at
Think wool is good for pulling over your eyes
    On this All Hallows Eve?

Smokey and the bandit

Zoe, Whiskey and Bimbo, the terrible trio
whatever happened to old Smokey?
He got left in the waiting room I think
with our little angel
the one whose nightdress caught fire

Setting out the mourning papers
we learnt to leave out the truth
forever braking hearts in The News of the World
all I did was help some joyrider
pull his car out of a ditch
peering over Hell's mouth and smoking Castellas

Completing a half marathon in record time with
Sebastian Coe
winning the men's on foot in the rain
racing down fore street off my trolley
losing out to the bandit queen

Foolish pride turning me down
love riding away as was my custom
accidentally through a swarm of bees
the time to fall was yet to come

Seductive opportunities lost to the bodyguard
seventeen seasons relegated to new year
unaware the recently canonised was in situ all along

Joining the Rollercoaster on tour
dreaming of our escape to the nineties
seeking out the Pavilions to see Jesus and the Mary Chain
I want to die in the USA! Popscene! Alright!
though I took cover at the bar from my bloody valentine
staying transfixed as the sunday joint rewound in a blur

Possessing Christian's Sunsolo a decade later
lighting paper aeroplane sorties up chimneys for a laugh
getting high and drinking Jim Beam
celebrating Kid A in South Park
The Strokes New York City Cops
Enkutatesh a new century year sowing the seed
for a moribund millennial creed

Well I'm holding out
for an eyeglass sonotone
one that can listen in
to those all seeing prescient voices I misheard

years ago.

Exclamation in ruin!

A Mad Hatter!
A Mercy Mission!
A Goosey Goosey Gander Show!
A Hand of Glory!
A Tanners Tale!
A Peasant Revolt!
An Apostles Hoody!
And Rasputin's Soliloquy!

Through the Looking Glass

If you could see what I can see
Would you want to be me?
No matter how high
You were always the one to let go

You left me in deep water
You turned the other cheek
Sink or swim in the mean streets
Where we all live and die

One fine day I'm going to find myself
On top of the world
But for now I'm just holding on
I'm just holding on to what I've got
I haven't got much and
The shoes I wear have done the walking
Now where I tread means more than today

As you ponder how you got this far
Through the Looking Glass
I see you and you see me
And the walrus displays your path
Come away with a call to speak your mind
And I promise the storm will pass

Wheel out those who you'd rather turn away
Not because of how they look
But because of what they say
Imagine yourself sitting by the roadside
You've got nothing but the clothes you wear
And all the busy people stop and stare
And turn a blind eye to what they see

And as you ponder how you got this far
Come away with a call to speak your mind
At the very least keep on the mean free path
And I promise to sow the seed

If you could see what I can see
Would you want to be me?
No matter how high
You were always the one to let go

You left me in deep water
You turned the other cheek
Sink or swim in the mean streets
Where we all live and die

One fine day I'm going to find myself
On top of the world
But for now I'm just holding on
I'm just holding on to what I've got
I haven't got much and
The shoes I wear have done the talking
Now what I said means more than today

Open Casting

The men of Fulan pitte
Scraped and racked to unload their precious cargoes
Between potholed puddles of slaking sand
Butting scaffold seams with embargoes
Structured to fit a scholars hand

Vortist wheels turned in unison by Blackwell's
Of tumbrel days in motion
Then stopped dead at Garsington Hall
No longer in want of pitted devastation; instead
Bequeathed to the Towers of Silence

Until the fate of the Lusitania was set
As the coal fires from the Titanic was learned
And the last glimpse of Shackleton's Endurance
Had been laid to rest in living memory

My White Rose

My White Rose
How far is it to Babylon?
Can I get there by train?
Yes. Jolly Jack be nimble
Almond Nick be quick
Beelzebub jump over the candlestick
Our phantom voices haunt the air
As we were still at play
Taking a swipe at Turkey snipe
Doctor Brown can hear them call and say

How far is Babylon?

silent running

A web of proclaimed disputes
That seek a vengeance remain
Wile others in temptation
Mire the silent breed
Bereft of reasoning
Abide this foolish creed

Thus, befalls upon a foe
Abroad. Bewildered and forlorn
Dream weavers go
Casting out shadows cursed
Plagued in hallowed wilderness
Where the silent running roam

Spun by wraths deathly hand
The solemn doubters tread
Upon blighted lands
The fallen sown
Coercing false sentiment
To dwelling places back home

So begins the days foretold
Beguiled with sullen face
These demons cold embrace
A dawning of a new formed race

No flame to rekindle anew
Just twisted broken forms
Torn.
Sinew by sinew

Bullet time

I shot a man
I killed a goose
I strangled a thief
I lynched a lone wolf
I used the same excuse
I kissed Monroe
I loved Garbo
I was James Dean's lover
Gary Cooper eat your heart out

Blind Funk

In the heart of Champagne country,
From the Battle of Dorking to the start of a new century
Marred by the passing of an Empress and the Julian calendar
(Not on my trench watch)
We'd hunker down from the Hotchkiss sheltering like troglodytes
Seasoned dwellers under fire from yellow cross air

High above from the twin towers Red Cross flags were flying,
A Cathedral sonority that couldn't help the dying
Bullies are curs at heart you know.
Calcining stones and blanching bones,
You can't foil an attempt to palliate an act of wanton vandalism
Sixty years before Philippe Petit bridged the gap
To dispense unctuous charm

When dinosaurs ruled the world in alarm,
When you suffered the palette of a home brew
When schoolboys were having mud baths in mixed up Harmignies
Between the trees, those killer trees Jack Johnson's fell harmlessly
Playing dead dog was our only alibi. Losing Grenville and Torridge,
Kingsley was the one loco that would not go amiss
Until Baden was rescued from midsummer losses at Scapa Flow

Our embittered cavalry always took charge,
Slicing their way through life like a knife through butter
A rear guard action lullaby in our own backyard
Defending Churchill's orders on poley cup day
Never mind the cacophony of smoke and thunder,
"What's the news on Gunboat Smith?"
A match made in heaven to score a ten in our favour

Then in one mad minute the weight on my shoulder,
Pulled me up, head down, upright over the top
Seeking to smote out the foe on Battle drawn lines
The triple alliance of blithe spirit arose, no hell could stop
Engaging a grey mass of blind funk suspended in a uniform sky
Leading swathes of rat infested infantry toward a souterrain cemetery
For that was our unquestionable duty in those teutonic times

To spin tall tales lent aside from fathers lies
To spit down the barrel of a gun spent from an Enfield rifle on leave
To slur the feint innocuous nature on suffragette city wives
To shun those whose emblem rent to tear the hearts from their sleeves
To suffer the patriotic fervour hell bent on costing us our lives

When I lost my hobnailed boot in the Duke of Marlborough's tree
When I took a slight drag from a Player's Navy Cut Cigarette
When I stole a kiss from Suzanne Valadon
When William Came

In the darkness to the beat of a dream

Upstares and Downstares

Perched on silver flattop
A chaffinch, nay a rook
Pecked a li'l 'ole in Fred's head
He was Lord Kitchener's cook

The maid baked a mighty broth
A quissop and a gand too hot
It was mulch two stringy for ever
The plasticine son of a pig's ear

Roger Bacon was sent forth
"Your perspective isn't even square"
Pre-empting the Draughtman's Contract
(Albeit Almuzlim in a darkened room)
By a bout of one thousand years

Flies became unwrapped
Bent down he tore right over old cock a snoop
Spoiling the Ministers soup
Splurting his lust over Nancy

Upstares and Downstares
And never the twain shall meat
There's nought more to laugh at more
Than a doubting Thomas in my book

A conscripted sprout on Sinai Mount
bye two Cretaceous prime intruders

A woll's a woll thar is n'doubt
One hundred thousand Hondurans grate
Relentless of high steam ahead
Many miles higher than for pity's sake
Even on Ever Testy so lofty to grant thee a grout

You guessed it Tenzing never put a flute wronged
As that spit in a frying pan of all the Kings ere
"Nay the woll's not arf as big" they chanted
(They don't rate himself for they are none the miser
no bigger than a grig)

Round and round the mulberry brush they rode
The wolls climbed higher and higher
"At this rate" Johnny shouted up "We'll reach
the Star Spaniel Bungler. Then we'll heave two
and attract ol' what's his name?"

Flu pip drove off in his delight.
Will ever grown men higher?

A woll's a woll thar is n'doubt
I can climb no higher
You donate land ere's thick for sale
Includes non-sticky pud
It's better than yer hanged mast left
Speciality alone this pile

(Mandalay wanders off the crevasses to gnaw everyone)

"Don't leave no stone upturned on Ever Testy
cos Spartans has never been shorn twice with spaghetti."

And that's a fact.

71

Sink or Swim

My All-Stars walk under a different canter
The Oxford Revue was not my alma mater

God is an actor
Jesus drives a tractor
Ploughs my field
I never yield

Wholesalers stole the seed now there's a no-one to feed
GM crops and fracking plots pulled out all of the stops

Plastics infiltrate our waters

halt the pain

Nitrate soils give no quarter

ease the strain

Poisons infecting our air

breathe with care

Climate causing a storm

before we're even born

Living on a knife-edge

keep away from the ledge

Ease the modern

make good the strife

Aerate

Life

Dumb Cake

It's another lavender morning
when the clocks turn back

see-saw rings around my eyes
flashbacks of love-lies-bleeding

scene through a lens on halloween
looking glass reflections in holy matrimony

red and black swallow stones charm you
finding out the birds and bees lived in boffies

a tansy prank led astray
the source of life so appealing

a dozen years of life spent dreaming
tempting glimpses, once caught stealing

newly ripe for St. Agnes eve meeting
tightly bundled until another leap years greeting

Seventh Heaven

Saved from the sea aged seven
Looking for a way passed heaven
Following the whispers and echoes of stone cairns
Marking the waves of reason
To tidal waft and wane in a safe haven
Hallowed be your name
In everything there is a season

Marching onwards to the shores
Drummer boys laid down the laws
'Wax with me tonight' I said
And we danced under the moonlight
For one last time I roared
And you caught the morning train
From the sea

Transit of Venus

On golden sands where we kissed
our footprints became fossilised in memory
the knot of your hair in my fingers
a tangle of eve to hold on to forever

we watched the sky begin to sleep
the sea wind blew across our backs
and the green flash found us wanton

there was juniper blossom in your hands
and that familiar scent lingered
until the shadows of the sun

carried you away

Rollin' in

Still deep within our winters sleep
Is the cusp of silent revolution
Sunk underneath heavy oceans
In keeping with the blackness of the deep

Oxford Street self

Tomorrow, you know
I'll lose myself
At a pedestrian highway

Overshadowing Marble Arch
and the Stop the War march
But I'm getting there
I'm getting there

Waiting.

For the Green Man's triumph
Centrepoint's sprawling pilgrimage
all
behind us

Charing Cross Foyle's
Bond Street spoils and
Soho perks after dark

It's all plane sailing
On a pedestrian highway

Tomorrow, you know
I'll lose myself

american Amsterdam

Have you heard the CIA are drinking tea
Under the English sun?
Did you ever wonder
How scene stealers took away
Spanish bullfighters Mom's?

In american Amsterdam
You know it's always the ones with the guns
Who know right from wrong
When the Queen's granddaughters rewrote
Charles Causley for fun

In a land of make believe
Where coincidence rings true
We circumnavigate the world and never get found
Is it strange enough for you?
So curious to know what went on inside the wardrobe
(Your Mother should know)

Living on an Island
Where the mad hatters can get out of jail for free
Dolled up to the nines sit down to a family meal
Your idle matters impress Her Royal Highness
Is sinking into dangerous seas

The things that mattered most
Have gone and flown away
Come with me on an ocean breeze
Climb aboard the Cutty Sark
We'll set sail down the Nile and
We'll see Cairo skyline in a short while

In a land of make believe
Where coincidence rings true
You raise a curtain wall to hide behind
But you can't pull down the blind and
Shower everyone with what you see
A well of loneliness removed for being obscene

In american Amsterdam
The GRU forge pictures on the King's Road
But they can't bring home the bacon
Crying alone in Nevermore Cathedral
The Queen's children got caught up in the lion's den
Waiting to join the hangers on

As we all tag along
In american Amsterdam

Poltergeist Thieves

What a heist from a poltergeist
robbing banks when no-ones looking
like Gremlins but you just can't see 'em
walking through walls
taking tea on the ceiling
casually pinching your pin
sneaking through virtual vaults
they spend it all
I don't know how
we let 'em do it
never owning up
to a table lifting séance trick
what a con don't you see?
it's nothing compared to this
has anyone cottoned on?
emptying your pockets
losing your money
business
your home
and job
to rob you
of self-respect
and dignity
laughing as they do
creating rag and bone
mankind
burning bearer bonds
an ounce in OZ
a yellow brick road
leading you on
a trounce on gold
no hope in growing old

in bitcoin sutures
taking a shit on our futures
taking a dump on our forefathers
hard work ethic
brothers and sisters in arms
a union struggle
a tonne of trouble
a dot-com bubble
to celebrate
let's inebriate
with a line of coke
a Tin Can Alley
of money men
laced with our fate
induced with poppers
to pork our chops
the fall of man
stooped in the gutter
a gutter snipe
eating tripe
selling you down the river
they trundle off to their old haunts
on ghost Islands overseas
like that one in LOST
that kept disappearing
and yet
it was all done
with cogs and wheels
sleight of hand
with
green screen
CGI

and a magic
key
not with
smoke and
mirrors
but in a dream
these poltergeists
who do the heist
are cunning individuals
they cover their tracks
leave only false stats
and leave you with no option
but to shrug your shoulders
on giants
whom we let down
now we regret
lest we forget
how we forgot
to inform ourselves
on the perils
of Olympic politics
were no Olympians
just mortal beings
losing our marbles
to lesser mortals
who have no morals
rest on our laurels
they grow on greed
we live on weed
consumer boom
what a carry on
FTSE nasdaq operators

Dow Jones possessed
in your living room
going live to feed
a tech-no-logical revolution
that takes the mickey
out of evolution
let's
spend a penny
let's buy a vote
let's lobby a goat
an empty tote
a nanny state
a helping hand
given all
given up
hand me a rope
l'll neknominate
who to down
everyone
let's giddy up
let's go to town
let's hang
the next government
I'll drown the lot
or better still
overthrow
this hung parliament
one

83

Outbound Life

Driven down Isolarion
Meeting with divinity
Voices sound like sand and glue
Wake me up I'm feeling blue

Another day passes me by
When I'm thinking of you
Summertime never lasts as long
When we were young
When friends were true
Year after year day by day
It's an outbound life were living

Gilded rails adorn the palace walls
And the London Eye looks down on us all
There goes another clean sweeper
Drenched to the bone out in all weathers
Whistling along to happy thoughts in his mind

Another day passes me by
When I'm thinking of you
Summertime never lasts as long
When we were young
When friends were true

Woken to a world so big
It's an outbound life were living
Year after year day by day
It's an outbound life
Living the dreams we once knew
Pulling us on

We can't be anything more

HER E
ENDETH
OXFORD
MILEHY
WAY
1667

Backword on the fly...

Buffalo Stance

Beware the Devil's pen of *parler librement*. A backword to when
protests erupted before Le Pen visited the Oxford Union. Local
newsagents were being threatened if they sold Hebdo papers,
back peddling on Theo van Gogh's freedom of expression as the
Lords listened in on demands to ban publications.

Je suis Charlie.

Laïcité and I hung back on the fly in a buffalo stance. Castaway
from my mind. I caught a meagre sense of a common strain of
thought to Oxon. Lost in the unveiling satire of *De Schreeuw.*
Night time alone breeds a different sense of ablution makes one
less prone to the drone of the latest laissez-faire scare tactics.
M&M's fell through my pockets. Leaving a trail of tic tacs.
Home brewed Morrell's on course. Sipping on a thirst of the local
view. It came from within Tom Tower. Wren was on a high.
Sandstones defrosted to a diffident feat. Triton frozen still indoors.
The Eagle and Child thawed bearing gifts in home comforts.
Gaz Coombes Matador tour enthralling once more at the Academy.
Gazebo tracks that travel beyond mere gestures of a clandestine
fact. Sweating profusely expressed dizzy aplomb.
Over lakes of Port Meadow bushel forth a single Perch concoction.
For a so-oh Aristotle like me operating thrice weekly Oxford Tube
futures. Going down to Jericho, sensing life anew alongside the
canal. News breaks as I walked passed the Tower of the Winds.
The heavens arose.
Opening up my heart in four directions. Flooding my nature.
Wandering solace to The White Rabbit. Ordering a pizza after re-
visiting Haddon's dip I sat refreshed in the listening corner with
The National. Graceless now, felt like sorrow.

Love is Enough

Shotover Ale to wash over a new found Windrush Love is enough.
As things are, Morris's arrow is camouflaged Warhol to the world.
Socialism is not for everyone that's why able pub-goers frequently
enjoy being social in front of the Wheatsheaf bar.
Just let me hear your voice...less.

The Commonwheal : William Morris 21st August 1886
Our comrades and friends are asked to bestic themselves to secure
freedom of speech in our public ways. In contradistinction to free-
dom of speech for certain classes and sects only. The spirit of soci-
alism is at war with class interests. Officialdom is giving it's supp-
ort to class interest only. For endearing to assert the right of free
speech the socialist legion has been heavily fined.

Burn after reading is less...useful.
Inherent Vice sprawled out from the Phoenix door onto a magic
carpet. "What's the hold up?" asked a ponytailed Pullman away
from his Dark Material rites. You would need an Amber Spy Glass
to view the Subtle Knife carving up a picture between Doc and
Bigfoot. Down in Topanga Canyon keeping the Myth of Sisyphus
hallucination at bay or could it be instilled within the salient artist
paranoia? Treading the boards with a best *plantar fasciitis* foot
forward. Maybe not if you need to visit the dark chiropractic arts
first. Owen Wilson the new escape artist from The Golden Fang.
Shia LaBeouf's Elastic Heart in a Saul Steinberg paper bag helps
to keep tabs on the Steppenwolf caged at bay. Not quite in the den
of The Grey. More Joseph Beuys with a coyote *I like America and
America likes me* and I still need that whisky.

Messengers of the Gods

I for one did not advocate paperweights as I slumped into Freuds.
Gloaming in the dew, fear stalking on my back.
Re-visiting ill nights from whooping cough could I hear the truth
in the zephyr wind?
Swearing in a large caffé Americano (with hot milk) stifled all my
concentrated thoughts but the feedback was mine.
'So Oh' rocked out Truck Stores Modern Nature's state.
Town Hall Art Fair were hosts of St. John the Baptist on a plate.
Shoemaker Levy can't help the screenplay for Ascending Jupiter in
literary three dimensions. Or the pollen count.
Dares you to ponder the likelihood it's mostly true. Bees are more
than honey.

Especially when they are small Messengers of the Gods.
Not that the local tramp brewing in the background noticed.
Something was rum here so I drank it.

Apprentice and Master

William Blake for goodness sake had all the answers.
He even dissed on Swedenborg which is telling.
Truth is nature.
Bodleian copperplate is bountiful as the saying goes.
But I'd be hard-pressed to quad-wrangle one from his wings.
Opportunities guaranteed to knock down Whistler's home.
William Blake's death mask came alive...we talked for a while.
He was prophetic. Imagining well above our intended status.
From grave machinations, to divine illuminations.
Clarity of the soul is mindful to the touch. I was moved onto a
rolling press. Bound inside No.13 Hercules Buildings.
May his resting place in Bunhills Cemetery be found.

(A new headstone was unveiled on August 12th 2018)
He was stacked well, but not in health.

Perfect Nonsense

St. Mary Magdalen bells were tuning in to the night scene.
An evenings red wine is the beacon of a temperate room.
So is Perfect Nonsense. A much better play on words.
Likened to saturation coverage when nothing has gone to plan.
Humour probably releases some aphrodisiac glue that I will
never need to decipher. (Or siphon off)
I'm rubber you're glue. Whatever you say bounces off me and
sticks to you.
Robert Webb nearly fell through the window as doors span around.
The butler made most of the changes even if she did timely undress.
Lamp shades, bonnets and tall mannequins epitomize three as the
magic number.
Laugh - so loud it felt good. Not in the middle of the night though.
That would be sheer unadulterated madness.

"But you know what this means don't you?
We are going to have to do the same thing all over again tomorrow."

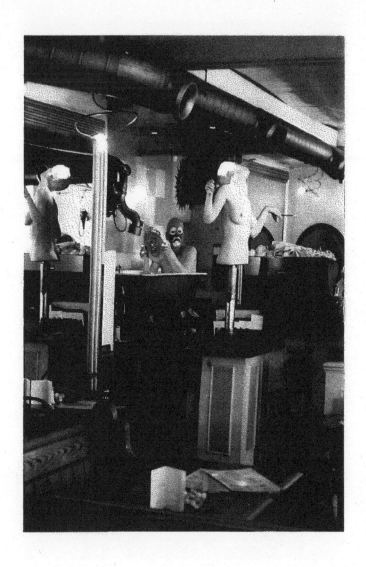

Claridge's

THE ULTIMATE
CUVÉE ROSÉ

CHAMPAGNE

Laurent-Perrier

MAISON FONDÉE
1812

Photo credit: Iris Veghe / Illustrator credit: Alice Drapanaski

ENJOY CHAMPAGNE LAURENT-PERRIER RESPONSIBLY

de qualité,

au service
de l'excellence.

*Your quality standards
for your best beef and lamb.*

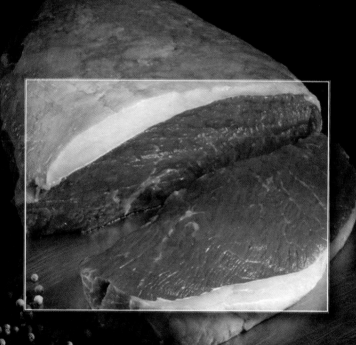

VIDEZ-VOUS LA TÊTE AVEC UN MAGAZINE QUI LA REMPLIT.

NOUVEAU
Vendredi
avec
Les Echos

Les Echos
WEEK-END

BUSINESS STORY / CULTURE / STYLE / ...ET MOI

CRU BOURGEOIS

www.chateau-brillette.fr

Moulis en Médoc

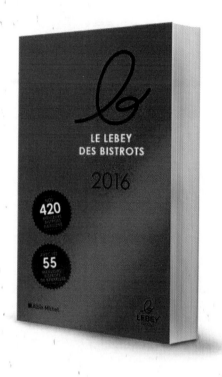

March 2016
Mars 2016

www.lebey.com

FERRANDI

L'ÉCOLE FRANÇAISE DE GASTRONOMIE
•
PARIS

Crédits photo : FERRANDI Paris, © 2015 Cook and Shoot by Aline Gérard

PARIS - JOUY-EN-JOSAS - BORDEAUX

GASTRONOMIE - MANAGEMENT

- Des formations du CAP au Bac + 5
- Des formations pour adultes, en reconversion professionnelle et en perfectionnement
- Des formations internationales
- Des cours pour amateurs

www.ferrandi-paris.fr

une école de la

CCI PARIS ILE-DE-FRANCE

les
LEBEY
de la
GASTRONOMIE
··········
2016

La soirée-trophée des Meilleures créations culinaires de l'année

11 avril 2016 - Pavillon Gabriel

Réservez dès maintenant

www.lebey.com

PARIS - LONDON

THE LEBEY RESTAURANT GUIDES

Le Guide des Restaurants de Paris
paraît tous les ans en novembre /
comes out in November of every year
Paris – London (new in 2015)
paraît tous les ans en novembre /
comes out in November of every year
Le Lebey des Bistrots de Paris et de Bruxelles
paraît tous les ans en mars / *comes out in March of every year*

www.lebey.com

Plus de 1200 adresses à Paris, Bruxelles mais aussi désormais
à Londres à connaître avec moteur de recherche avancée et
toute l'actualité des restaurants ou bistrots.
*Over 1200 venues to discover in Paris, Brussels and now London
too, with an advanced search engine and the latest news on
restaurant and bistros.*

LES 3 GUIDES LEBEY EN **VERSION MOBILE** / *THE MOBILE PHONE VERSION OF THE 3 LEBEY GUIDES*

Les meilleures adresses de Paris, Bruxelles et désormais Londres
sur votre smartphone avec géolocalisation et
moteur de recherche par critères.
*The best addresses in Paris, Brussels and now London,
available on your smartphone, with GPS and search facilities using
selected criteria.*

Pour nous contacter / *To contact us*:
Lebey.com

LE LEBEY PARIS - LONDON

Plus de 200 adresses où bien manger à Paris & Londres

Over 200 recommendations for quality dining in Paris & London

EDITORIAL

Chers Amis,

Jamais deux capitales n'ont pris autant de plaisir à se comparer. À table, Paris déploie ses grandes adresses historiques ou met en avant sa bistronomie quand Londres dépêche ses chefs devenus stars médiatiques ou mise sur ses gastropubs pour prétendre, chacune à leur façon, au titre de scène mondiale de la gastronomie. Dans cette guerre aussi fratricide que médiatique, il était temps qu'un guide réunisse les adresses où il est possible de décemment déjeuner ou dîner dans chacune des deux destinations. En évitant les restaurants prestigieux qui n'ont pas besoin de nous pour communiquer, comme les lieux trop à la mode qui privilégient le look au détriment du bien manger. Aussi, avons-nous été aussi basiques qu'un estomac errant dans les rues de Londres ou de Paris, désirant partager un peu de chère locale ou goûter une franche cuisine, de préférence de saison. Et, pour rendre notre sélection encore plus appétissante et évidente, nous avons mis l'accent sur la viande. Où diable faut-il aller pour se sustenter de généreuses pièces de bœuf ou de morceaux de choix d'agneau, que précéderont ou suivront pulled pork (effiloché de porc) ou terrine maison, tarte pas forcément tatin ou crumble de saison ? Ces deux capitales attirant un nombre croissant d'hommes d'affaires ou de touristes, et réunissant une population de plus en plus hétérogène, ce guide, voulu dans les deux langues, vient réconcilier des deux côtés de la Manche les épicuriens du quotidien. Sans oublier les Londoniens qui habitent Paris ou vice et versa, ni les Parisiens qui travaillent à Londres ou vice et versa, voire les Parisiens et Londoniens qui ne connaissent toujours pas les pépites culinaires de leurs villes respectives. N'hésitez pas à consulter ce guide dans tous les sens, à le lire dans les deux langues comme à franchir allégrement arrondissements ou districts, il comporte pas moins de deux cents adresses que nous avons toutes visitées. Depuis presque trente ans (*), les Guides Lebey ont imposé avec succès leurs exigences et modes de sélection à Paris, visitant chaque adresse au moins une fois l'an et obligeant ses enquêteurs incognito à payer leurs notes. Reconnaissez, qu'il était temps que Londres profite à son tour de la touche Lebey !

(*) Le *Guide Lebey des Restaurants de Paris* et le *Lebey des Bistrots* existent depuis 1987.

EDITORIAL

Dear friends,

Never have two capital cities been so keen to compare themselves. When it comes to eating, Paris unfurls with pride its grand historic restaurants and tradition of bistros, whilst London brandishes its media star chefs or gastro pubs, both cities claiming, in their own right, a central place on the international gastronomic stage. In this fratricidal, media war, it was high time that a guide list all those restaurants where a good meal can be had in each of the two cities. We have not included the prestigious restaurants which have no need of our guide for marketing purposes, or the latest "in" places which place more emphasis on décor than the quality of their food. We simply played the part of an empty stomach, wandering through the streets of London or Paris, hoping to share some local dishes or taste some unpretentious, preferably seasonal, food. And, to make our selection even clearer and more tempting, we focused on meat dishes. Where are the best places to enjoy generous joints of beef or prime cuts of lamb, with slow-cooked, pulled pork or a home-made terrine to start or follow, and a selection of tarts or pies or a crumble made from fruit in season? Since both capitals attract an increasing number of businessmen and tourists, with increasingly cosmopolitan populations, this bilingual guide aims to bring together food-lovers on both sides of the Channel. Not forgetting those Londoners who live in Paris, or vice versa, nor the Parisians who work in London, or indeed those Parisians and Londoners who have yet to discover the gastronomic treasures of their respective cities. Feel free to use this guide as you see fit, to read it in both languages and to explore happily the various districts or areas which are included. It contains no less than two hundred addresses which have all been tested. The Lebey restaurant guides have imposed their rigorous selection methods for over thirty years (*), inspecting each venue at least once a year, and requiring their incognito food critics to pay for their meals. You have to admit that it was about time that London got its own taste of Lebey!

(*) The *Guide Lebey des Restaurants de Paris* and the *Lebey des Bistrots* have been around since 1987.

SOMMAIRE /
TABLE OF CONTENTS

Les 101 meilleurs bistrots de Paris /
The 101 best bistros in Paris

Les 102 meilleurs bistrots ou gastropubs de Londres / *The 102 best bistros or gastro pubs in London*

Index

NOTRE PALMARÈS DES BISTROTS /
OUR TOP-CHOICE OF BISTROS

SYMBOLES / *SYMBOLS*

 Une bonne cuisine de bistrot /
Good bistro food

 Une très bonne cuisine de bistrot /
Very good bistro food

 Un des meilleurs bistrots /
One of the best bistros

 Les meilleurs bistrots de l'année /
The best bistros of the year

PARIS

🍲 LE **BEEF CLUB**
58, rue Jean-Jacques Rousseau, 75001 Paris
Métro / *Tube* : Étienne Marcel – Les Halles
+33 (0)9 54 37 13 65
www.eccbeefclub.com

Maintenant que le Fish Club voisin a changé de fonctions (espace privatisable), le Beef Club continue de défendre la cause des amateurs de viande dans ce quartier Montorgueil toujours aussi vivant. Quelques tables dans la rue, un décor de charcuterie reconvertie en bistrot branché 20-35 ans (avec discothèque au sous-sol !), certes pas un parangon de service ou de gastronomie, mais, avec notre copieux os à moelle et notre tartare tout préparé, nous n'avons pas boudé notre plaisir et la carte des vins n'est pas sans intérêt.

Now that the Fish Club next door operates differently (it can be booked for private functions), the Beef Club continues to defend the cause of meat lovers in the lively Montorgueil neighbourhood. A few tables outside in the street, the décor of a charcuterie converted to a trendy bistro for 25 to 30 year olds (there is a disco downstairs), not exactly a paragon of good service or gastronomy, but we enjoyed our generous bone marrow and our prepared steak tartare, also the wine list is quite interesting.

À la carte : 12 € • Carpaccio de bœuf, keen's cheddar, huile de noisette et raifort / *Beef carpaccio, Keen's cheddar, walnut oil and horseradish* 13 € • Tarte citron / *Lemon tart* 10 € • Profiterole / *Profiterole* 10 €.
Fermé le samedi et le dimanche au déjeuner / *Closed Saturdays and Sundays for lunch.*

🍲 HEIMAT

37, rue de Montpensier, 75001 Paris
Métro / *Tube* : Palais Royal – Musée du Louvre
+33 (0)1 40 26 78 25
www.heimatparis.com

Une nouvelle création de Pierre Jancou, le barbu télévisuel (il passa comme une comète) qui fut à l'origine de Racines, Vivant et autres établissements à succès. A priori, une signature plus que recommandable pour cette table de rez-de-chaussée, distribuée en petites salles, dont le caractère séraphique tient avant tout à une absence totale de décor et à un habillage de pierres apparentes. Ce qui permet de se concentrer sur des produits de belle qualité, apprêtés de manière harmonieuse, ce qui ne gâte rien. Et toujours ces petits bémols, aisément rectifiables dans le cas de légumes en quantité infinitésimales avec notre plat, en revanche plus difficiles à faire comprendre en matière de vins... La sélection, ample, est entièrement vouée aux vins « vivants », auxquels le personnel est tellement habitué, qu'il n'est même plus capable de se rendre compte que le nôtre était totalement oxydé (goût de xérès) !

A new creation of bearded TV chef Pierre Jancou (seen briefly on the air) who also started Racines, Vivant and other successful venues. An excellent "signature" for this street level restaurant, with its small dining rooms and a seraphic atmosphere due to its total absence of décor and exposed stone walls. This allows one to focus on the high quality ingredients, prepared in a harmonious way. There are always small mistakes that are easy to rectify, like the vegetables, served in a miniscule portion with our dish. It's more complicated to talk to the staff about the wines. The large selection is entirely focused on "living" wines, that the staff are so used to that they are no longer capable of recognizing that ours was completely oxidized (it tasted like Sherry) !

Menus / *Prix fixe menu* : 50 €, 70 € (dîner / *dinner*).
Fermé les midis, le dimanche et le lundi toute la journée / *Closed Sundays, Mondays and for lunch.*

🍲 PIROUETTE

🍲 5, rue Mondétour, 75001 Paris
🍲 Métro / *Tube* : Étienne Marcel
+33 (0)1 40 26 47 81
www.oenolis.com

Dans ce coin presque calme des Halles, il faut souligner la qualité des travaux engagés pour faire de cette adresse un rendez-vous des plus agréables. Hauteur sous plafond, mezzanine plus intime (mais hélas bruyante), somptueux bar en bois blond et tables dressées sur une pittoresque terrasse dès les beaux jours. Enfin, des assiettes précises, des dressages avenants, une cuisine d'inspiration bistrotière mais largement revisitée avec un talent indiscutable placent Pirouette dans l'antichambre des grands établissements que le chef a d'ailleurs fréquentés. Jolie carte des vins avec des choix judicieux grâce à la complicité de Jean-Marie Fréchet associé du lieu et œnologue réputé (Œnolis).

In this almost calm area of Les Halles, the quality of the work undertaken to make this place a most pleasant venue, deserves to be pointed out. High ceilings, an intimate (but noisy) mezzanine, a sumptuous pale wood bar and tables set out on a picturesque terrace as soon as the weather permits. And last but not least, precise dishes, attractively presented, a bistro style cuisine largely revisited with unfailing talent, put Pirouette neck and neck with gastronomic restaurants, which is where the chef received some of his training. An attractive wine list with judicious selections, thanks to the complicity of renowned oenologist Jean-Marie Fréchet, who is a partner of this establishment.

À la carte : Effiloché de canard, navets marinés, pickles orange / *Shredded duck, marinated turnip, orange pickle* 14 € • Cèpes, châtaignes caramélisées, amandes / *Cepe mushrooms, caramelized chestnuts and almonds* 25 € • Ris de veau et crème à l'ail, légumes du marché / *Sweetbreads with garlic cream, seasonal vegetables* 22 € • Saint-jacques, céleri fondant, piments doux et kakis / *Scallops, tender celeriac, sweet Pepper and persimmon* 22 € • Tarte café, glace panais et vanille, poire / *Coffee tart, parsnip and vanilla ice cream, pear* 12 € • Ossau-iraty et sa confiture de cerises noires / *Ossau Iraty cheese and its black cherry jam* 10 €.
Menus / *Prix fixe menu* : 40 € (déjeuner / *lunch*), 60 € (dîner / *dinner*).
Fermé le dimanche / *Closed Sundays*.

🥟 AU VIEUX COMPTOIR

17, rue des Lavandières Sainte-Opportune, 75001 Paris
Métro / *Tube* : Châtelet – Pont Neuf
+33 (0)1 45 08 53 08
www.au-vieux-comptoir.com

Un simple bistrot dans les parages Châtelet-Les Halles avec son mobilier d'origine (chaises et tables) et son atmosphère à faire fuir les modeux du quartier. Excepté que la maison, menée par une patronne sympathique et volubile, affiche une solide sélection de vins, propose de remarquables charcuteries (boudin, terrine, pâté en croûte, saucisse, sublime jambon blanc, etc., confectionnés par le patron, vite disert si vous l'interrogez) et offre des assiettes aux portions d'un autre temps (les entrées ont la taille d'un plat !). À mettre sous globe pour tant de générosité affichée.

A simple bistro in the Châtelet-Les Halles area, with its authentic furniture (tables and chairs) and an atmosphere that scares off the neighbourhood fashionistas. Except that, run by a friendly, chatty "patronne", it boasts a solid selection of wines and remarkable charcuterie (black pudding, terrine, pâté en croûte, sausage, wonderful cooked ham, etc, prepared by the "patron" who is more than happy to talk about them) and offers dishes in portions rarely seen nowadays (the starters are as big as a main course !). Hopefully, this exceedingly generous place will remain just as it is.

À la carte : Foie gras de canard, piment d'Espelette / *Duck foie gras with Espelette chilli* 15 € • Couteaux poêlés en marinade / *Pan fried marinated razor clams* 12 € • Boudin noir maison / *Home made black pudding* 18 € • Ravioles pecorino menthe / *Pecorino and mint ravioli* 25 € • Paris Brest / *Paris Brest pastry* 10 €.
Menus / *Prix fixe menu* : 23 €.
Fermé le dimanche et le lundi / *Closed Sundays and Mondays.*

🥘 A. NOSTE

🥘 6 bis, rue du 4 Septembre, 75002 Paris
🥘 Métro / *Tube* : Bourse
+33 (0)1 47 03 91 91
www.a-noste.com

A. Noste, « chez nous » en patois landais. Chez qui ? Chez Julien Duboué. Passé par le feu médiatique de l'émission Top Chef, ce jeune chef talentueux décline son amour pour les Landes, en offrant dans un seul et même lieu, trois concepts gastronomiques. Au rez-de-chaussée, à gauche, une estafette (oui, oui !) distribue ses taloas (galette basque maison pressée comme un panini), près du bar central, les assiettes de tapas (délicieuses) valsent dans un joyeux brouhaha. À l'étage, le calme reprend le dessus dans une salle à manger au décor épuré, orné d'orchidées. La cuisine à demi ouverte dévoile fièrement sa rôtissoire, thème central du restaurant. Ici, pas de carte mais un menu dégustation à trois plats le midi et six le soir. La plupart des produits viennent du Sud-Ouest et les viandes caramélisées à souhait sont découpées à table et servies à volonté. Un paradis pour carnassiers !

A. Noste, "our place" in patois from the Landes. Who's place? Julien Duboué's. After being on the Top Chef TV show, this young and talented chef declares his love to the Landes region by offering 3 gastronomic concepts in the same venue. At street level, on the left, his taloas (Basque style Panini) are served from a van, near the bar in the middle, the delicious tapas plates circulate in a joyous brouhaha. The first floor dining room, with its understated décor and orchids is much more peaceful. The half-open kitchen shows off the rotisserie, the main theme of the restaurant. Dishes are not offered "à la carte", instead there is a set tasting menu, with three courses for lunch and six for dinner. Most of the ingredients come from the Southwest of France and the delightfully caramelized meats are sliced at the table and you can eat as much of them as you like. Heaven for meat lovers !

À la carte : Escabèche de thon grillé à la japonaise / *Grilled tuna escabèche japanese style* 15 € • Curry de gambas crémeux, pommes vertes et coriandre fraîche / *Creamy shrimp curry, green apples and fresh coriander* 12 € • Ravioles au foie gras et gingembre / *Foie gras and ginger ravioli* 19 € • Couteaux et moules

à la plancha, vinaigrette basquaise / *Razor clams and mussels « a la plancha » with a Basque vinaigrette* 14 € • Chou vanillé, caramel au beurre salé / *Vanilla cream puff, salty butter caramel* 8 € • Figues rôties au gingembre et crème de cassis / *Roasted figs with ginger and crème de cassis* 8 €.
Ouvert tous les jours / *Open every day.*

🍽 FRENCHIE BAR
🍽 6, rue du Nil, 75002 Paris
🍽 Métro / *Tube* : Sentier
　+33 (0)1 40 39 96 19
　www.frenchie-restaurant.com

....

Il suffit de jeter un coup d'œil sur la prolixe carte des flacons pour s'assurer que l'appellation « bar à vins » est amplement méritée pour ce « Frenchie », sis en face du restaurant du même nom. Cette carte fait bien sûr la part belle aux grandes appellations (puligny-montrachet, châteauneuf-du-pape, côte-rôtie, pauillac, etc.), mais son intérêt majeur consiste à faire découvrir d'excellents viticulteurs dans des terroirs moins prestigieux (Savoie, Auvergne, Hérault...). L'assiette pourtant ne ressemble en rien à ce qui est trop souvent proposé dans ce type d'établissements : une cuisine inspirée, innovante et sophistiquée fait vite oublier les vagues planches de charcuterie ou de fromages parfois jetées en pâtures aux amateurs de bars à vins. L'excellent Grégory Marchand a installé ici un vrai « restaurant à vins », son « Brittany blue lobster roll », sandwich au homard fondant et goûteux également servi au « Frenchie to go », le « take-away » voisin, est une pure merveille ! Dommage qu'il nous faille patienter parfois si longtemps pour s'asseoir à une table que les règles locales interdisent de réserver par avance...

A glance at the prolific wine list is all one needs to be convinced that this "Frenchie", right opposite the eponymous restaurant, is a proper wine bar. Naturally it offers a wide selection of the best appellations (puligny-montrachet, châteauneuf-du-pape, côte-rôtie, pauillac, etc.), but more interestingly it allows one to discover excellent wine makers in less prestigious regions (Savoie, Auvergne, Hérault...). What you'll find on your plate is nothing like the food that is too often served in this kind of establishment. Here you have an inspired cuisine, innovative and sophisticated, that makes you quickly forget the platters of indifferent charcuterie or cheeses that are usually tossed casually at wine bar amateurs. The excellent Grégory Marchand has established here a true "wine restaurant". His mouth watering "Britanny blue lobster roll", also on the menu at the nearby "Frenchie to go", is simply wonderful ! It's a shame that one often has to wait a very long time to get a table, as the local rules don't allow for reservations…

À la carte : Ventrêche de porc de Bigorre, pane carasau, romarin / *Bigorre pig ventresca, pane carasau, rosemary* 12 € • Caille, crémeux de pommes de terre, artichaut / *Quail, creamy mashed potatoes, artichoke* 18 € • Merlu, petits pois, pamplemousse / *Hake, peas, grapefruit* 16 € • Coleslaw de seiche fumée, carottes, pignons de pin, olives kalamata / *Smoked cuttlefish coleslaw, carrots, pine nuts, Kalamata olives* 14 € • Tarte amandine aux abricots, glace aux herbes / *Amandine apricot tart, herb ice cream* 9 € • Panna cotta au sureau, cerises, sablé breton / *Elderberry panna cotta, cherries, Breton shortbread* 9 €.
Fermé au déjeuner, le samedi et le dimanche / *Closed for lunch, Saturdays and Sundays.*

LES ENFANTS ROUGES

9, rue de Beauce, 75003 Paris

Métro / *Tube* : République – Temple

+33 (0)1 48 87 80 61

A la tête des Enfants Rouges depuis un an et demi, le chef Daï Shinozuka - ancien de chez Camdeborde - ne se repose pas sur ses lauriers. Il continue de nous régaler avec des propositions classiques (délicieux pâté de campagne maison) tout en nous étonnant avec de subtiles touches de créativité (salicorne et citron vert râpé en garniture d'une succulente poitrine de veau...). Ses assiettes élégantes et plus techniques qu'il n'y paraît font des Enfants Rouges un des meilleurs bistrots de la capitale. On regrette seulement le choix trop limité de vin au verre (seulement quatre !).

> *Since chef Daï Shinozuka - who worked for Yves Camdeborde - took over the Enfants Rouges, he hasn't exactly been resting on his laurels. He keeps on delighting us with his classical preparations (delicious home made country pâté) while surprising us with his subtle touches of creativity (samphire and grated lime served with a succulent veal breast). His elegant and understated technical dishes make Les Enfants Rouges one of the best bistros in the capital. Our only regret is the limited selection of wine by the glass (only four !).*

Menus / *Prix fixe menu* : 35 € (déjeuner / *lunch*, semaine / *week*), 40 € (dîner / *dinner*).
Fermé le mardi et le mercredi / *Closed Tuesdays and Wednesdays*.

🚇 LE METROPOLITAIN

🚇 8, rue de Jouy, 75004 Paris
🚇 Métro / *Tube* : Saint-Paul
+33 (0)9 81 20 37 38
www.metroresto.fr

Dans un décor joliment vintage à base d'anciennes banquettes de métro en bois et de carreaux de faïence blancs aux murs, Paul-Arthur Berlan délivre une cuisine astucieuse, plaisante et gourmande. Ancienne star de la télé-cuisine (demi-finaliste Top Chef 2011 sur M6), il charme d'abord les yeux par de belles assiettes structurées et colorées, façon « bistro-visuelle », avant de surprendre en bouche par des assemblages croustillant-fondants ou encore viandes et fruits, concoctés à base d'excellents produits choisis chez les amis du patron. Le bonheur est là, dans cette petite rue calme du Marais tranquille, service aussi efficace qu'enjoué.

In a charming vintage décor, with old wooden metro seats and white faience tiles on the walls, Paul-Arthur Berlan, produces a clever, pleasing and flavourful cuisine. Former TV star chef (semi finalist of Top Chef in 2011), he starts by enchanting your eyes with colourful structured dishes, in a "visual bistro" style, and then surprises your mouth with crunchy-tender textures or meat and fruit pairings, prepared with top quality ingredients, selected from producers who are also friends of the owner. True happiness can be found in this calm little Marais street. The service is as jolly as it is efficient.

À la carte : Cuisses de grenouille, crème de persil, émulsion à l'ail / *Frogs legs, parsley cream, garlic emulsion* 18 € • Cannelloni de tourteau, pomelos et mayonnaise relevée au curry / *Crab cannelloni, pomelo and curry mayonnaise* 14 € • Tourte feuilletée, canard colvert et foie gras, réduction de gibier / *Duck and foie gras puff pastry pie, venison reduction* 24 € • Blanquette de joues de lotte au lait de coco / *Monkfish cheek, coconut milk blanquette* 24 € • Sphère meringuée, marron myrtilles, crème glacée au yaourt / *Meringue sphere, chestnut and blueberries, frozen yoghurt* 10 € • Poire pochée à la vanille, crème puits d'amour gratinée / *Vanilla poached pear, puits d'amour cream "au gratin"* 10 €.
Menus / *Prix fixe menu* : 24 € (déjeuner / *lunch*), 39 € (dîner / *dinner*).
Fermé le samedi midi et le dimanche / *Closed Saturdays for lunch and Sundays.*

L'AGRUME

15, rue des Fossés-Saint-Marcel, 75005 Paris
Métro / *Tube* : Les Gobelins
+33 (0)1 43 31 86 48
www.restaurantlagrume.fr

Décoration contemporaine et un brin impersonnelle, cuisine ouverte autour de laquelle on peut s'attabler pour voir s'affairer un chef précis, concentré et peu loquace, service souriant et attentif mais lui aussi peu bavard, musique très feutrée. Tout est ici mis en scène pour inviter à se concentrer sur l'assiette, plus « gastronomique que bistrotique », et sur la carte, qui fait la part belle aux produits de la mer, ancrée dans la tradition mais capable de l'adapter avec subtilité et finesse au goût du jour par touches impressionnistes.

A slightly impersonal contemporary décor, an open kitchen one can sit around and observe the quiet and focused chef, smiling and attentive waiters, who are also not very talkative, very soft music. Everything here is organised to make you concentrate on your dishes, which are more gastronomic than "bistronomic", and on the menu which offers a wide selection of sea food dishes, rooted in tradition, but recreated with subtle impressionist modern touches.

À la carte : Tartare de bar lié à la chair de tourteaux, citrons et radis / *Sea bass and crab tartare, lemons and radishes* 22 € • Assiette de jambon ibérique pata negra / *Plate of Spanish pata negra ham* 14 € • Côte de veau rôtie et champignons à la crème / *Roasted veal chop and mushrooms in cream* 34 € • Pavé de bar poché, étuvée de poireaux et tartare d'huîtres / *Sea bass steak, stewed leeks and oyster tartare* 34 € • Panna cotta vanillée et jus de framboises / *Vanilla panna cotta and raspberry juice* 6 € • Soupe de cerises, chantilly et tuiles / *Cherry soup with Chantilly cream and tuiles* 8 €.
Menus / *Prix fixe menu* : 25 € (déjeuner / *lunch*), 45 € (dîner / *dinner*).
Fermé le dimanche et le lundi / *Closed Sundays and Mondays*.

 AT BAR À VINS

4, rue du Cardinal Lemoine, 75005 Paris
+33 (0)1 56 81 94 08
www.atsushitanaka.com

Atsushi Tanaka a aménagé la cave de son petit établisse-
ment et créé un espace voûté, très calme, dévolu aux vins.
Le choix, en la matière, est court (une dizaine de réfé-
rences) mais original, et l'essentiel réside en fait dans la
possibilité de déguster, à côté de charcuteries de qualité,
des assiettes issues directement de la carte de dégustation
de son restaurant. Évidemment, cela vole haut, en raison à
la fois de la finesse des apprêts et de la subtilité des assai-
sonnements qui laissent pantois. Ne manquez pas, s'il est
encore à la carte, le bœuf, topinambour et foin, une petite
merveille !

*Atsushi Tanaka has converted the cellar of his small res-
taurant and created a peaceful vaulted space devoted to
wine. The selection is limited (around ten wines) but it
is original, and more importantly it allows one to taste -
along with some charcuterie - dishes from the tasting
menu of the restaurant. These are all extremely refined,
with sophisticated preparations and subtle seasonings
that take one's breath away. If it's still on the menu, don't
miss out on the beef, Jerusalem artichoke and hay. It's
quite wonderful !*

À la carte : Boudin noir Bellota / *Bellota black pudding* 12 € •
Jambon de bœuf wagyu / *Wagyu beef ham* 18 € • Bœuf, topi-
nambour, foin / *Beef, Jerusalem artichoke, hay* 16 € • Gambas à
la plancha / *Prawns "à la plancha"* 20 € • Merlu au bouillon de
bulots / *Hake with whelk broth* 25 € • Pomme-sauge / *Apple-sage*
12 €.
Fermé les midis et le mardi toute la journée / *Closed for
lunch and Tuesdays.*

LE BISTRO DES GASTRONOMES

10, rue du Cardinal Lemoine, 75005 Paris
Métro / *Tube* : Cardinal Lemoine – Jussieu
+33 (0)1 43 54 62 40
www.bistrodesgastronomes.com

Ce bistrot élégant repris il y a trois ans par Cédric Lefèvre
(ex Bistrot Volnay et disciple de Christian Constant) ne

manque pas de caractère. Dans la décoration soulignée de noir tout d'abord, dans la cuisine qui ose les assaisonnements corsés ensuite et tout simplement dans la personnalité bien trempée de ce chef qui sait où il veut emmener ses clients. Et ça tombe bien car nous avons beaucoup de plaisir à le suivre... Le menu-carte met à l'honneur les beaux produits et les saveurs affirmées et, en saison, ose proposer deux préparations de lièvre à la royale, celles d'Ali Bab (alias Henri Babinsky) et du sénateur Couteau. Les deux goûtées l'année dernière nous avaient comblés. Service timide mais prenant de l'assurance au fil du temps.

This elegant bistro, which was taken over a few years ago by Cédric Lefèvre (ex Bistrot Volnay and disciple of Christian Constant), oozes character. This is noticeable first in the décor, underlined in black, then in the dishes with their flavourful seasonings and last but not least, in the strong personality of this chef who knows where he wants to take his clients. We're happy to follow him...The prix-fixe menu features quality ingredients and bold flavours and, when it's in season, dares to offer two versions of "lièvre à la royale" (a traditional dish with hare), that of Ali Bab (a.k.a. Henri Babinsky) and that of the senator Couteau. We tasted both last year and were enchanted. The service is on the shy side but gaining in confidence.

Menus / *Prix fixe menu* : 30 € (déjeuner / *lunch*), 40 € (dîner / *dinner*).
Fermé le samedi midi, le dimanche et le lundi / *Closed Saturdays for lunch, Sundays and Mondays.*

🍲 LE **BON SAINT-POURÇAIN**

🍲 10 bis, rue Servandoni, 75006 Paris
Métro / *Tube* : Mabillon
+33 (0)1 43 54 93 63

Entre Saint-Sulpice et Luxembourg, dans une ruelle qui signe le chic de la rive gauche, voilà certainement la meilleure défense et illustration du bistrot contemporain : décor limpide et revisité années cinquante, carte simple et restreinte, prix clairs et service aussi efficace que bienveillant. Le jeune chef, Mathieu Techer, sélectionne avec un même bonheur ses produits qu'il cuit à la perfection viandes ou poissons, prépare ses légumes ou monte ses sauces. De l'incontournable duo poireaux/œuf mollet (à redécouvrir avec sa vinaigrette d'arachide) au baba humidifié (et surtout pas noyé dans l'alcool), un sans faute très prometteur. Belle carte des vins, dont un champagne brut nature étonnant. Petite terrasse pour les beaux jours.

Between Saint-Sulpice and Luxembourg, in a chic left-bank side street, this is most definitely one of the best representatives of a contemporary bistro : 50s style understated décor, simple short menu, transparent prices and a staff that is as efficient as it is friendly. The young chef, Mathieu Techer, takes as much pleasure in selecting his ingredients as he does in cooking them to perfection, both meat and fish, as in preparing his vegetables or his sauces. From the "signature" leek with soft boiled egg (to be rediscovered with its peanut oil vinaigrette), to the moist baba (not drowned in alcohol), a promising "sans faute". Nice wine list, including a surprising champagne brut nature. Little terrace for sunny weather.

À la carte : Poireaux vinaigrette d'arachide, œuf mollet / *Leeks in a peanut oil vinaigrette, soft boiled egg* 9 € • Tomate ancienne, mozarella pistou / *Heirloom tomato, mozzarella, pesto* 10 € • Quasi de veau Desnoyer champignons blettes / *Desnoyer veal rump, mushrooms, Swiss chard* 24 € • Merlu rôti fenouil pommes de terre blettes / *Roasted hake, fennel, potatoes, Swiss chard* 24 € • Baba au rhum, ananas, espuma coco / *Rum baba, pineapple, coconut espuma* 9 €.
Fermé le samedi et le dimanche / *Closed Saturdays and Sundays.*

🥟 FREDDY'S

🥟 54, rue de Seine, 75006 Paris
Métro / *Tube* : Mabillon – Odéon – Saint-Germain-des-Prés

Déjà à la tête du Sémilla, Éric Trochon, chef de cuisine, Meilleur Ouvrier de France, a investi le pas-de-porte voisin pour créer son second établissement. Pas de réservation, pas de téléphone et même... pas de table. En lieu et place, des mange-debout, un zinc, des comptoirs, des tabourets et, au milieu, une cuisine ouverte sur la salle avec moult barbecue et plancha. Pas de menu non plus, mais une carte de plats miniatures à commander en donnant son prénom et à savourer en fonction de ses envies, de son appétit, du style de préparation ou de cuisson souhaité (grillade, plancha, croustillant, à tartiner, salaison...etc.) Pour compléter la collation, deux bouchées sucrées tout aussi réussies mais aussi un saint-nectaire ou un chaource à se damner et à apprécier avec le pain sorti tout droit du four du boulanger d'à côté (Cosi).

Already in charge of Sémilla, chef Eric Trochon, a "Meilleur Ouvrier de France", has taken over the next-door shop to create his second venue. No reservations, no phone and... no tables. Instead, there are high tables, a bar, counter-tops, stools, and in the middle, an open kitchen, with many barbecues and planchas. No menu either, but a list of small plates, that one orders by giving one's first name, choosing them according to one's taste, appetite, the style of preparation or cooking (on the grill, à la plancha, crisped, spreadable, cured... etc.). To finish off the meal, two sweet spoonfuls that are just as delicious, and also mouth-watering Saint-Nectaire or Chaource cheeses, to be enjoyed with the bread just out of the neighbouring baker's oven (Cosi).

À la carte : Arancini aux escargots / *Snail arancini* 6 € • Accras sauce chien / *Accras, spicy sauce "chien"* 6 € • Rillons de veau de Clem / *Clem's veal cured* 8 € • Enoki et panchetta / *Enoki mushrooms and pancetta* 4 € • Aileron de volaille, miel, soja / *Honey soy chicken wing* 7 €.
Ouvert tous les jours / *Open every day.*

🥮 JOSÉPHINE (CHEZ DUMONET)

🥮 117, rue du Cherche-Midi, 75006 Paris
🥮 Métro / *Tube* : Duroc – Falguière
  +33 (0)1 45 48 52 40

....

L'un des derniers bistrots à jouer la tradition à la perfection. Cadre historique inespéré car resté dans son jus, service appliqué et diligent, et plats réalisés avec une rigueur et une technique qui ne sont plus hélas enseignées dans les écoles hôtelières. Le foie gras offre un bel équilibre de saveurs, le foie de veau est servi rosé à la perfection et la tarte aux pommes feuilletée à souhait. Carte des vins abondante et pointue, et avec un peu de chance vous aurez peut-être la possibilité de visiter la cave que gère avec maestrio l'inénarrable maître des lieux. Et, d'ailleurs, que deviendrait Paris sans Jean-Christian Dumonet ?

One of the last bistros that upholds tradition to such a degree of perfection. It offers an unchanged historic décor, diligent and attentive service, dishes prepared with a rigour and technique that are sadly no longer taught in catering school. The foie gras is a model of well-balanced flavours, the calf's liver is cooked to perfection, and the apple tart light and crispy. The wine list is plentiful and selective, and if you're lucky you might get to visit the cellar, which the owner, who is quite a character, manages with brio. What would Paris become without Jean-Christian Dumonet?

À la carte : Morilles farcies / *Stuffed morels* 24 € • Confit de canard maison / *Home made duck confit* 23 € • Millefeuille de pigeon et ses cuisses confites / *Pigeon millefeuille with the preserved leg* 34 € • Saint-jacques aux pousses d'épinard / *Scallops with baby spinach* 28 € • Millefeuille Jean-Louis / *Millefeuille à la Jean-Louis* 14 € • Tarte fine chaude aux pommes / *Warm apple tarte fine* 12 €.
Fermé le samedi et le dimanche / *Closed Saturdays and Sundays.*

L'AFFABLE
10, rue de Saint-Simon, 75007 Paris
Métro / *Tube* : Rue du Bac
+33 (0)1 42 22 01 60
www.laffable.fr

Après d'importants travaux en cuisine et un toilettage efficace en salle, ce bistrot s'impose plus que jamais comme l'adresse à la fois gourmande et confortable du quartier. À la carte, des produits nobles travaillés avec beaucoup de sérieux et en même temps d'à-propos, des notes végétales toujours bienvenues et un vrai sentiment de bien-être. Encore un dernier petit effort sur la carte des vins, et la prestation sera parfaite. Accueil chaleureux et tarifs élevés en dehors du menu du déjeuner.

After an extensive renovation of the kitchen and an efficient sprucing up of the dining room, this bistro is more than ever the delicious and relaxing "place to be" in the neighbourhood. On the menu, you'll find quality dishes that are prepared in a serious and coherent manner, with welcome vegetal overtones, that give a true feeling of wellbeing. A little work on the wine list and everything will be perfect. A warm welcome and steep prices outside of the lunch menu.

À la carte : Cuisses de grenouille, sésame à la sauge, pancetta / *Frogs legs, sesame with sage, pancetta* 14 € • Langoustines, mangue, poivre du Népal / *Langoustines, mangoes, Nepal pepper* 19 € • Entrecôte d'Argentine, grenaille, gingembre / *Argentinean rib steak, baby potatoes, ginger* 35 € • Saint-pierre, fenouil, salicornes / *John dory, fennel, samphire* 28 € • Soufflé chocolat / *Chocolate soufflé* 15 € • Cheese-cake concombre, verveine / *Cucumber and verbena cheesecake* 14 €.
Menus / *Prix fixe menu* : 28 € (déjeuner / *lunch*).
Fermé le samedi et le dimanche / *Closed Saturdays and Sundays*.

🍽 LE BELHARA

🍽 23, rue Duvivier, 75007 Paris
🍽 Métro / *Tube* : École Militaire
+33 (0)1 45 51 41 77
www.bistrotbelhara.com

Installé depuis maintenant deux ans à cette nouvelle adresse, Thierry Dufroux a su - à en entendre les commentaires des tables voisines ! - conquérir une clientèle exigeante. Ceci grâce à une cuisine reposant sur des produits typiquement « bistrotiers » travaillés avec beaucoup de justesse (délicate épaule de lapin, merlu divinement bien cuit...). Le service chaleureux et efficace ainsi que de généreuses attentions (succulentes guimauves maison avec le café...) contribuent à faire encore et toujours du Belhara une table toute aussi excellente qu'agréable !

Thierry Dufroux who took over here more than two years ago, has – from the sound of the neighbouring tables – managed to win over a demanding clientele. This is thanks to his cuisine, based on typical "bistro" ingredients, precisely prepared (delicate rabbit shoulder, marvellously cooked hake...). The efficient and friendly service, as well as some nice little surprises (yummy home made marshmallows with the coffee...) help to make the Belhara a delicious and delightful place to enjoy a meal.

À la carte : Foie gras de canard des Landes confit dans sa graisse, figues mi-sèches / *Duck foie gras from the Landes, semi-dried figs* 18 € • Fin velouté de cèpes, crème montée et lard croustillant / *Delicate cepe mushroom soup, with whipped cream and crispy bacon* 12 € • Cœur de ris de veau cuisiné au beurre blanc demi-sel, pommes de terre purées / *Heart of sweetbreads, cooked with a salty butter "beurre blanc", mashed potatoes* 35 € • Daurade royale française accompagnée de son risotto carnaroli, poêlée de champignons, ail, persil, vieux Ossau Iraty / *French gilthead bream with Carnaroli risotto, pan fried mushrooms, garlic, parsley, aged Ossau Iraty cheese* 21 € • Chocolat noir truffé à la feuille d'argent, craquelin nougatine, glace au caramel / *Black chocolate with silver leaf, crispy nougatine, caramel ice cream* 10 € • Riz au lait à notre façon / *Rice pudding our way* 10 €.
Menus / Prix fixe menu : 34 € (déjeuner / *lunch*), 38 € (dîner / *dinner*)
Fermé le dimanche et le lundi / *Closed Sundays and Mondays*.

🥟 CHEZ GRAFF
🥟 62, rue de Bellechasse, 75007 Paris
🥟 Métro / *Tube* : Solférino
+33 (0)1 45 51 33 42

....

Salle tout en longueur, murs vert d'eau, parquet blond, vieilles photos n&b encadrées, tables et chaises (confortables) en bois clair, banquettes : le décor est chic, épuré, chaleureux. Le chef, un japonais passé par l'Astrance, envoie une cuisine hexagonale, aux saveurs nerveuses (sauces de pomme verte ou de persil), colorée, faisant la part belle aux légumes. Les touches asiatiques sont rares (marinade au miso), plus évidentes dans les dressages : le carpaccio de veau évoque un lac de lotus ! Formules réduites et prix doux au déjeuner ; le soir, la carte, plus étoffée, est complétée par des charcuteries et fromages basques. Bon choix de vins. Accueil très sympathique.

A long dining room with sea green walls, a light wood floor, old black and white framed photographs, light wood (comfortable) chairs and tables : the décor is elegant, understated and welcoming. The chef, who is Japanese and has worked at Astrance, prepares a colourful, lively (green apple or parsley sauces) French cuisine with a definite focus on vegetables. The Asian touches are rare (miso marinade), more apparent in the presentations : the veal carpaccio conjures up a lotus lake! Short menus and affordable prices at lunchtime. In the evening, the menu offers a wider selection of dishes as well as Basque charcuterie and cheeses. Good wine selection. Very welcoming.

À la carte : Burrata à la truffe noire / *Burrata with black truffle* 15 € • Soupe de Potimarron / *Pumpkin soup* 9 € • Bavette Aberdeen-Angus marinée au miso / *Aberdeen-Angus rib steak in a miso marinade* 19 € • Ceviche de bar / *Sea bass ceviche* 9 € • Paris-brest / *Paris-Brest pastry* 9 € • Mousse au chocolat / *Chocolate mousse* 8 €.
Menus / *Prix fixe menu* : 25 € (déjeuner / *lunch*, semaine / *week*).
Fermé le dimanche / *Closed Sundays*.

🍽 LE MARLOE

🍽 12 rue du Commandant Rivière, 75008 Paris
🍽 Métro / *Tube* : Saint-Philippe-du-Roule
+33 (0)1 53 76 44 44
www.marloe.fr

Un bistrot gastronomique à l'évidence car tous les plats ici servis sont réalisés à partir des mêmes produits et avec la même attention que ceux proposés à l'Arôme, table voisine et réputée... Aussi le croque-monsieur ne trouve pas d'équivalent à Paris, comme le plateau de fromages est assez sérieux pour en faire tout un repas. Et puis on aime bien ici le soin apporté autant dans la carte façon grignotage (assiette de charcuterie, beignets, terrine de gibier...) que dans les plats plus traditionnels (remarquable blanquette à base de ris de veau). La sélection de vins se montre tout aussi prometteuse (avec un choix de vins au verre dès cinq euros) et le service a gardé le professionnalisme des grandes maisons tout en se montrant proche et chaleureux...

This is most definitely a "gastro-bistro". All the dishes are prepared with the same ingredients and the same care as those of L'Arôme, a nearby renowned restaurant...The croque-monsieur has no equivalent in Paris and the cheese platter is a meal in itself. We like the fact that things on the snacking menu (charcuterie platter, beignets, venison terrine...) are prepared with as much attention as the more traditional dishes (remarkable blanquette with sweetbreads). The wine selection also shows great promise (with wines by the glass starting at 5 €) and the service is top-notch yet friendly and welcoming.

Menus / *Prix fixe menu* : 36 €, 44 €.
Fermé le samedi et le dimanche / *Closed Saturdays and Sundays.*

🍲 BOUILLON

🍲 47 Rue de Rochechouart, 75009 Paris
Métro / *Tube* : Anvers – Cadet – Poissonnière
+33 (0)9 51 18 66 59
www.restaurantbouillon.fr

....

Serait-ce le retour en force d'une cuisine de tradition dans cet arrondissement réputé jusque-là pour ses tables créatives, voire aléatoires, ou pour ses adresses ultra-spécialisées ? En tous cas, sous un niveau sonore élevé et dans un cadre mignonnet (parquet, tables bois, coloris vert d'eau et blanc), Marc Favier, nourri à l'écurie Piège, offre des plats aussi classiques (bouillon, canette et faux-filet à partager, etc.) qu'émouvants ou même excitants, dont on avait parfois perdu la trace. Un retour à saluer, épaulé par ailleurs par un choix de vins ample, en particulier en bourgognes et languedocs.

Is traditional cuisine making a comeback in this arrondissement known up to now for its creative, sometimes unreliable or ultra-specialised venues? Anyway, in a noisy, cutie-pie setting (wood floor, wooden tables, pale green and white colours), Marc Favier, trained in the Piège "stable", offers dishes that are at the same time traditional (broth, duckling and sirloin steak to share, etc), moving or even exciting, that had by and large disappeared. A comeback to be applauded, backed up by a large selection of wines, in particular Burgundies and Languedocs.

À la carte : Bouillon de vrais champignons de Paris, foie gras de canard, céleri-coriandre, vinaigre fumé / *Broth of real champignons de Paris, duck foie gras, celery-coriander, smoked vinegar* 14 € • Merlu de ligne, cuit sur l'arête, potiron écrasé, sauce suprême / *Line caught hake, cooked on the bone, pumpkin mash, "suprême" sauce* 25 € • Gâteau au chocolat de mon apprentissage, crème montée / *Chocolate cake from my days as an apprentice, whipped cream* 10 € • Tarte aux pommes, crème double Borniambuc / *Apple tart, double Borniambuc cream* 9 €.
Fermé le dimanche et le lundi / *Closed Sundays and Mondays.*

🥧 CAILLEBOTTE

🥧 8, rue Hippolyte-Lebas, 75009 Paris
🥧 Métro / *Tube* : Cadet – Le Peletier –
Notre-Dame-de-Lorette – Saint-Georges
+33 (0)1 53 20 88 70

Bois clair, pierre, marbre au comptoir, fonte, ampoules à filaments, larges baies vitrées, cuisine vitrée largement visible de la première salle : digne d'une revue de déco, le Caillebotte porte beau. La cuisine, reprenant celle de la maison mère (Le Pantruche), est largement en phase avec une carte dans l'air du temps, métissant produits et garnitures (concombre et pêche jaune, œuf mollet et blanc de seiche...), le plus souvent avec bonheur. On aime en particulier le recours à des produits trop souvent négligés (merlu, maquereau...), les plats très construits associant plusieurs éléments, l'attention portée aux légumes. Bonne carte des vins avec des vins au verre à prix raisonnable. Pain de Poujauran. Bon café. Accueil sympathique et service rapide.

With its light wood, marble bar, cast iron fixtures, incandescent light-bulbs, large windows, and opened glass kitchen largely visible from the first dining room : the décor at Caillebotte definitely belongs in an interior design magazine. The cuisine, which takes after that of its "parent" restaurant (Le Pantruche) is definitely in synch with the times, mixing and matching ingredients (cucumber and peach, soft boiled egg and cuttlefish...) most often with very satisfying results. We like their use of ingredients (hake, mackerel...) that are often overlooked, their very structured dishes bringing together an array of ingredients, the attention they give to vegetables. Good wine list with reasonably priced wines by the glass. Bread from Poujauran. Good coffee. A warm welcome and efficient service.

À la carte : Tomates anciennes et aile de raie au basilic / *Heirloom tomatoes and skate wing with basil* 11 € • Gaspacho andalou, chair de tourteau et avocat / *Gaspacho from Andalucia, crabmeat and avocado* 11 € • Pigeon vendéen rôti, galette de maïs et cébettes snackées / *Roasted pigeon from Vendée, corn cake and charred green onions* 21 € • Filets de maquereaux de Saint-Gilles Croix-de-vie / *Mackerel fillets from Saint-Gilles Croix de Vie* 21 € • Mûres cassis, fromage blanc vanillé, crumble / *Blackberries, blackcurrants, vanilla fromage blanc, crumble* 9 € •

Nage de pêche jaune, glace marjolaine, meringue / *Peach "à la nage", marjoram ice cream, meringue* 9 €.
Menus / *Prix fixe menu* : 35 € et 49 € (dîner / *dinner*).
Fermé le samedi et le dimanche / *Closed Saturdays and Sundays.*

🍲 FLESH
25, rue de Douai, 75009 Paris
Métro / *Tube* : Blanche
www.flesh-restaurant.com

Avant même de pousser l'huis, on sait où l'on met les pieds : Barbecue Bar est inscrit en façade, profession de foi confirmée à la lecture de la carte, avec poulet fermier, black angus, travers de porc fumé, voire filet de merlu... travaillés selon ce mode de cuisson et avec trois sauces possibles. L'ensemble, proposé sur des tables bois clair, sous un réjouissant fond sonore sixtie's (Doors, Byrds, Neil Young...) et concocté par un chef américain, se révèle tout-à-fait convaincant dans sa simplicité.

Even before going inside this bistro, you know what you're going to get : Barbecue Bar is posted on the outside. This is confirmed by the menu, with free-range chicken, black angus beef, smoked spare ribs, or even filet of hake... all cooked accordingly, with a choice of three sauces. All this, served on light wood tables, to a cheerful soundtrack from the sixties (the Doors, the Byrds, Neil Young...) and cooked by an American chef, is pleasingly simple.

Fermé le dimanche soir / *Closed Sundays for dinner*.

🍲 L'OFFICE
🍲 3, rue Richer, 75009 Paris
🍲 Métro / *Tube* : Bonne Nouvelle
+33 (0)1 47 70 67 31
www.office-resto.com

Parmi les qualités que l'on attend d'un restaurant - et à laquelle nous sommes particulièrement attentifs et sensibles - c'est la régularité, et la capacité à maintenir dans la durée un niveau élevé de qualité. Sans mollir. Depuis plusieurs années, L'Office relève ce défi. Et même si, depuis son ouverture, plusieurs cuisiniers se sont succédés dans ce joli bistrot, au décor simple et net, le propos reste clair : proposer une cuisine créative mais juste, recevoir avec courtoisie, et être assez malin et élégant pour n' être ni branché, ni has been. Une jolie adresse qui semble incarner à elle seule une certaine idée de la gastronomie parisienne de ce début de siècle : renouvelée mais solide, simple mais exigeante.

One of the qualities one expects from a restaurant – and one that we really look for and appreciate – is consistency, and the ability to keep a high level of quality over time, without fail. For the last few years, L'Office has been rising to the challenge. Even if different chefs have cooked in this attractive bistro, with its simple décor, the message remains clear : to serve a tested yet creative cuisine, with courtesy, and to be clever and elegant enough to be neither trendy nor has-been. A lovely place, that seems to embody what Parisian gastronomy should be in this new century : reinvented yet reliable, simple but demanding.

Menus / *Prix fixe menu* : 28 € (déjeuner / *lunch*), 34 € (dîner / *dinner*).
Fermé le samedi et le dimanche / *Closed Saturdays and Sundays*.

🍲 LE PANTRUCHE

🍲 3, rue Victor Massé, 75009 Paris
🍲 Métro / *Tube* : Pigalle
+33 (0)1 48 78 55 60
www.lepantruche.com

Un vieux bistrot de Paname resté dans son jus, un peu à l'étroit dans ses murs (une trentaine de couverts) d'autant qu'il semble connu de tous les guides touristiques étrangers. On y savoure une sage cuisine de ménage discrètement modernisée, mais peut-être moins percutante qu'au Caillebotte, son « bébé ». Pain de Poujauran. Vins bien choisis et belle sélection au verre. Réservation souvent indispensable.

An unchanged retro-style Paris bistro, it can be a little cramped (it seats around 30 people), especially as it seems to be known to all the tourist guidebooks. Here you will enjoy home-style cooking, discreetly updated, but not quite as bold as that of Caillebotte, the newly opened restaurant by the same team. Bread from Poujauran. Well chosen wines with a good selection by the glass. It is often necessary to book a table in advance.

Menus / *Prix fixe menu* **:** 35 € (dîner / *dinner*).
Fermé le samedi et le dimanche / *Closed Saturdays and Sundays.*

🍲 RICHER
🍲 2, rue Richer, 75009 Paris
🍲 Métro / *Tube* : Bonne Nouvelle – Cadet – Poissonnière

Un stolon du restaurant l'Office voisin en version bistrot/ brasserie. Larges baies vitrées claires, pierres grattées jusqu'à l'os, banquettes comme des divans profonds... On peut y passer sa journée, dès potron-minet pour le petit déj', grignoter tapas, tartines ou tortillas au fil des heures, faire salon de thé dans l'aprèm', s'arsouiller de bière pression ou de superbes eaux-de-vie en after... En tout cas ne pas manquer les repas : assiettes malicieuses et goûteuses, mariant de nombreux ingrédients, équilibrant différentes textures (rôti, confit, crème, purée, émulsion, braisage...). Bons produits et cuissons justes. Belle carte des vins « à la mode » de l'Office. C'est-à-dire qu'il n'y a pas de classement - hors la couleur -. Millésimes, pays, appellations, prix, cuvées, sont mélangés : « pour que le client ne se laisse pas aller à ses habitudes » dit-on à l'Office... Conséquence : il faut prendre le temps de lire ligne à ligne les différentes pages... ou s'en remettre au choix du service pour les vins au verre... Cela se limite alors à un « blanc ou rouge ? » et à un verre apporté sans mentionner l'appellation ou le millésime... Bon pain du Grenier à Pain voisin. Carte d'eaux-de-vie. Accueil sympathique ; service rapide. Pas de réservation, pas de téléphone.

A "cousin" of L'Office a nearby restaurant, in a more bistro/brasserie style. With its large windows, light stonework, bench seats that are like deep couches...you could spend all day here, from early morning breakfast, to snacking on tapas, tartines and tortillas throughout the day, sipping afternoon tea, downing a beer or an after-dinner eau de vie...But most of all, you should have a proper meal, with its clever tasty dishes, mixing and matching many ingredients, textures (roasted, preserved, creamy, puréed, emulsionned, braised...), quality products and precise cooking. A good wine list, in the style of "L'Office", which means that nothing is organized other than by colour. Vintages, countries, appellations, prices and cuvees are all mixed together. So that clients don't cling to their habits, according to the people at L'Office... So you'll have to take your time and read each line of the different pages...or ask for advice for wines by the glass. In which case you'll be asked if you want red or white and brought a glass with no mention of its vintage or appellation...Good bread from the nearby Grenier à Pain. List of "eaux de vie". A warm welcome and efficient service. No reservations. No telephone.

À la carte : Maquereaux, betterave au vinaigre de framboise et écume escabèche / *Mackerel, beetroot in raspberry vinegar and escabèche emulsion* 9 € • Consommé champignons, foie gras poché, crème de raifort et nouille de riz / *Mushroom consommé, poached foie gras, horseradish cream and rice noodles* 10 € • Canard rôti confit, purée de chou-fleur, shitake confit au figue 18 € • Joue de bœuf braisée, panais rôtis meunière et échalotes confites au raisin / *Braised beef cheek, roasted parsnips "meunière" and shallots cooked with grapes* 17 € • Dorade poêlée, purée de carottes, noix de cajou et émulsion citronnelle / *Pan fried gilthead bream, carrot purée, cashew nuts and citronella emulsion* 18 € • Crème brûlée chocolat au lait, glace passion et croquant noisette / *Milk chocolate crème brûlée, passion fruit ice cream, and hazelnut crisp* 8 € • Pommes caramélisées, crumble yaourt, crème épaisse et sorbet céleri branche / *Caramelized apples, yogurt crumble, crème fraiche and celery sorbet* 8 €.
Ouvert tous les jours /*Open every day.***

🍲 ALBION

🍲 80, rue du Faubourg Poissonnière, 75010 Paris
Métro / *Tube* : Poissonnière
+33 (0)1 42 46 02 44

Dans une chouette ambiance tamisée de bar à vin décontracté, avec ses caisses de vins à l'entrée, ses tables sans nappes en quinconces et sa cuisine ouverte au fond... une équipe souriante, à dominante anglo-saxonne, délivre une cuisine punchy et sexy où les textures et les saveurs s'entrechoquent avec une réussite certaine. Ah ! ces langues d'oursins recouvertes de crème de maïs. Oh ! cette purée de betterave confite venue avec son chèvre frais épouser un rôti de porc Bellota. Et que dire de ce crémeux de chocolat dynamité par des éclats de crumble cacao et de fruits de la passion ! Tout est bon chez Albion, succulent même. Mais attention, sans formule, ni menu, au déjeuner comme au dîner, la note grimpe assez vite...

In a softly lit, happy, relaxed, wine bar atmosphere, with its cases of wine at the entrance, its bare tables and its open kitchen in the back, an Anglo-Saxon team serves up a punchy sexy cuisine where textures and tastes collide successfully. Ah ! the sea urchin tongues covered in a corn cream. Oh ! The purée of slow cooked beetroot with its fresh goat cheese, paired with Bellota pork roast. And what could one possibly add when tasting the chocolate "crémeux" blown away by the cacao crumble and passion fruit! Everything at Albion is good, succulent even. But beware that, as there is no prix fixe menu for lunch or dinner, it can be quite expensive...

À la carte : Ceviche de bar de ligne, avocat, cervelle de canut / *Sea bass ceviche, avocado, herbed cream cheese* 12 € • Onglet de bœuf, cèpes poêlés, purée d'oignon et d'ail, crème de raifort / *Top skirt steak, pan fried cepe mushrooms, onion and garlic purée, horseradish cream* 22 € • Filet de canette, crème de panais, crumble de parmesan / *Duck filet, parsnip cream, parmesan crumble* 19 € • Cabillaud aux pistaches, choux de Bruxelles glacés aux coquillages, crème de cresson / *Cod with pistachios, Brussels sprouts cooked with shellfish, cream of cress* 23 € • Assiette de fromages fermiers bios, poire conférence pochée au vin rouge / *Plate of organic farm cheeses, pear poached in red wine* 13 € • Poire comice caramélisée, crème glacée mascarpone, crumble

aux amandes / *Caramelized pear, mascarpone ice cream, almond crumble* 8 €.
Fermé le samedi et le dimanche / *Closed Saturdays and Sundays.*

ANCIENNE MAISON GRADELLE
8, rue du Faubourg-Poissonnière, 75010 Paris
Métro / *Tube* : Poissonnière
+33 (0)1 47 70 03 23
www.anciennemaisongradelle.com

Un décor neuf mais qui donne l'illusion (réussie !) de l'ancien pour une maison qui ne manque pas de caractère. Plafond à caissons, miroirs mouchetés et sol en pierre font bon ménage dans ce restaurant piloté par Stéphane Gilard, un ancien du Plaza. La carte est axée sur la viande et la volaille et les plats traditionnels exécutés avec soin. Le menu du midi à 26 € est une affaire, le pain croustillant et délicieux de Rodolphe Landemaine, le café en provenance de la brûlerie de Belleville et le chocolat qui l'accompagne de Jean-Paul Hévin. Nombreux whiskies et une trentaine de vins à la carte. Personnel attentif et souriant.

This restaurant, oozing character, has a new décor that (successfully !) gives the impression of being vintage. The coffered ceiling, speckled mirrors and stone floors go well together. At the helm is Stéphane Gilard, who worked at the Plaza. The menu puts the emphasis on meat, poultry and carefully executed traditional dishes. The 26 € lunch menu is a bargain. The crispy and delicious bread is from Rodolphe Landemaine, the coffee is from the brûlerie de Belleville, and the chocolate that is served with it comes from Jean-Paul Hévin. A large selection of whiskies and 30 wines on the wine list. Attentive and cheerful staff.

À la carte : Œuf de poule, artichaut, champignons et parmesan / *Hen's egg, artichoke, mushrooms and parmesan* 11 € • Gîte à la noix de bœuf, betteraves et vinaigrette onctueuse / *Round steak, beetroots and smooth vinaigrette* 14 € • Côte de bœuf Aberdeen Angus (pour 2) / *Aberdeen Angus prime rib (for 2)* 90 € • Noix d'entrecôte d'Argentine, frites maison / *Argentinean rib steak, home made chips* 33 € • Brioche perdue, glace vanille et zestes confits / *Brioche French toast, vanilla ice cream and preserved zests* 11 € • Clafoutis confiture de la maison aux cerises ou aux pruneaux, glace au kirsch / *Clafoutis, home made cherry and prune jam, kirsch ice cream* 10 €.

Menus / *Prix fixe menu* : 38 € (dîner / *dinner*).

Fermé le samedi midi et le dimanche / *Closed Saturdays for lunch and Sundays*.

LA GRILLE

80, rue du Faubourg-Poissonnière, 75010 Paris
Métro / *Tube* : Poissonnière
+33 (0)1 47 70 89 73

Avant d'être le premier gastropub de Paris, cette Grille a construit sa réputation sur son beurre blanc qu'au déjeuner comme au dîner il faisait bon déguster dans les deux salles adjacentes qui fleuraient le Paris nostalgie. Fin d'une époque, les travaux entrepris ont préservé quelques éléments architecturaux et prétexté de la présence du bar aussi imposant que pittoresque pour proposer une sélection de bières comme il en existe peu à Paris. Le turbot au beurre blanc est toujours à la carte, entouré de quelques autres plats traditionnels à partager (tourte, côte de bœuf...). En fait, cette nouvelle Grille nous plaît bien car elle fait une heureuse synthèse entre hier et aujourd'hui, et s'amuse à donner par petites touches un peu d'humour, à qualifier bien entendu d'anglais, dans le décor comme dans le service. Une réussite pour l'atmosphère et pour cette volonté de bien faire tant au niveau de la carte des boissons que des plats servis.

Before becoming Paris's first gastropub, the Grille built its reputation on its "beurre blanc" that one could enjoy for lunch or dinner, in the two adjacent dining rooms with their nostalgic Paris atmosphere. End of an era, the renovation has left some of the architectural features and used the impressive bar as an excuse to serve a selection of beers rarely seen in Paris. The turbot with "beurre blanc" is still on the menu, with a few other traditional dishes to be shared (pie, beef rib...). We quite like this updated Grille, which happily brings together the past and the present, and shows a gentle sense of humour - British of course - in the décor as well as the service. A success, both

*in its atmosphere and the effort put in to make the drinks
list and the dishes just right.*

À la carte : Os à moelle rôti, salade de mâche, cornichon et persil
plat / *Roasted bone marrow, lamb's lettuce, pickle and flat leaf
parsley salad* 12 € • Tourte de volaille, salade verte / *Chicken pie,
green salad* 15 € • Poitrine de cochon de montagne laquée, purée
de patate douce / *Glazed mountain pork belly, sweet potato mash*
33 € • Tarte tatin minute, crème épaisse de vache Jersiaise (à
partager) / *Tarte Tatin (to share)* 18 €.
Menus / *Prix fixe menu* : 19 € (déjeuner / *lunch*).
**Fermé le samedi midi et le dimanche / *Closed Saturdays for
lunch and Sundays.***

☕ RATAPOIL

🍽 72, rue du Faubourg Poissonnière, 75010 Paris
Métro / *Tube* : Cadet – Grands Boulevards – Poissonnière
+33 (0)1 42 46 30 53
www.ratapoildufaubourg.fr

Trois associés, peut-être même amis, ont ouvert avec beau-
coup de bonheur cette adresse du Faubourg. Ils ont réuni
leurs compétences et leurs moyens, pas de décorateur mais
au contraire un accrochage réussi et personnel de toiles
achetées au cours de ventes ou sur les brocantes. Atmos-
phère chaleureuse tant au déjeuner qu'au dîner, et carte
tout aussi personnelle et engagée avec un menu très acces-
sible à midi et des plats tous facturés à dix euros le soir pour
un repas à composer selon ses envies et ses disponibilités.
Cuisine efficace autour de produits bien choisis, assiettes
simples mais redoutablement gourmandes et carte des vins
en devenir avec des vignerons plus partenaires que fournis-
seurs. Vous l'avez compris, ce Ratapoil réinvente avec verve
et intelligence le bistrot du faubourg.

*Three partners, most likely friends, opened this success-
ful place on the Faubourg. They gathered their skills and
resources and chose not to use an interior decorator, but
rather to hang on the walls a personal selection of paint-
ings bought in auctions or at flea markets. A warm atmos-
phere at lunch as well as dinner, a personal and sincere
menu with a very affordable prix-fixe for lunch and dishes
all priced at 10 € in the evening that you can mix and
match as you please. The ingredients are well chosen and*

carefully prepared, the dishes are simple yet irresistibly appetizing. The wine list is a work in progress with wine makers who are more like partners than suppliers. As I'm sure you've understood, Ratapoil is reinventing the Faubourg bistro with brio and intelligence.

À la carte : Vapeur d'huîtres, couteaux et coques, écume de la mer / *Steamed oysters, razor clams, clams, sea emulsion* 10 € • Filet de veau teriyaki caramélisé servi froid, carottes de couleur / *Caramelized teriyaki veal filet served cold, multicoloured carrots* 10 € • Chartreuse de joue de cochon, foie gras, truffes et jus corsé / *Pork cheek chartreuse, foie gras, truffles and flavourful jus* 10 € • Millefeuille de pied et épaule de cochon, crème de boudin noir / *Millefeuille of pig trotter and shoulder, black pudding cream* 10 € • Coings rôtis et crème anglaise / *Roasted quince with crème anglaise* 10 € • Tarte à la rhubarbe et crème au citron / *Rhubarb tart with lemon curd* 10 €.
Menus / *Prix fixe menu* : 22 € (déjeuner / *lunch*).
Fermé le samedi midi et le dimanche / *Closed Saturdays for lunch and Sundays.*

🍲 AUBERGE PYRÉNÉES CÉVENNES
🍲 106, rue de la Folie-Méricourt, 75011 Paris
Métro / *Tube* : République
+33 (0)1 43 57 33 78

Il faut venir ici autant pour Françoise qui gère sa salle avec son franc-parler et surtout son irrésistible faconde que pour la belle et généreuse cuisine que Daniel son mari défend avec autant d'application que d'amour. Le couple a beaucoup travaillé pour faire de cette auberge un lieu incontournable pour qui cherche encore à Paris un lieu aussi authentique et chaleureux. La clientèle connaît de nombreuses stars, et on s'en fiche totalement car c'est bien notre couple d'aubergistes qui, le temps d'un repas, mérite les projecteurs. On vous aime !

You should visit this place as much for Françoise who runs the dining room with her outspoken manner and her irresistible glibness, as for the lovely and generous cuisine that her husband Daniel prepares with both dedication and love. The couple worked hard to make this place a sure-fire success with anyone searching Paris for an authentic welcoming restaurant. There are many stars among the clients, but no matter, since it's most definitely our couple of restaurateurs who deserve, for as long as the meal lasts, to be in the spotlight. We love you !

À la carte : Foie gras frais de canard / *Fresh duck foie gras* 23,30 € • Lentilles / *Lentils* 7,70 € • Foie de veau à la lyonnaise / *Lyonnaise style calf's liver* 28,80 € • Quenelle de brochet sauce nantua / *Quenelle with Nantua sauce* 19,80 € • Tarte Tatin / *Tarte tatin* 8,20 € • Vacherin maison / *Home made vacherin* 10,40 €.
Menus / *Prix fixe menu* : 31 €.
Fermé le samedi midi et le dimanche / *Closed Saturdays for lunch and Sundays.*

🍲 BISTROT PAUL BERT
🍲 18, rue Paul Bert, 75011 Paris
🍲 Métro / *Tube* : Faidherbe-Chaligny
+33 (0)1 43 72 24 01

Une institution bistrotière, au point qu'elle a essaimé deux annexes dans la même rue, l'Écailler du Bistrot et le 6, Paul Bert. Grâce à Bertrand Auboyneau aux commandes, rien ne manque une nouvelle fois à notre bonheur : des plats traditionnels généreux et bien tournés, un excellent rapport qualité/prix, une atmosphère vivante et colorée, sans oublier une carte des vins exceptionnelle, avec plusieurs centaines de références. Le cadre se compose de trois salles dans leur jus, avec de vieilles affiches, des tables au touche-touche et un grand bar dans l'entrée. Il faut prendre son mal en patience avant de pouvoir s'attabler, tant l'endroit est populaire et ne désemplit pas. Mention spéciale aux frites, coupées au couteau, qui comptent parmi les meilleures servies dans un restaurant parisien. Service sur les dents, zigzaguant de table en table.

A genuine Paris institution, it now boasts two offspring in the same street : L'Ecailler du Bistrot and the 6 Paul Bert. Thanks to Bertrand Auboyneau, the man in charge, we get to enjoy generous traditional dishes, excellent value for money, a lively colourful atmosphere and an exceptional wine list, with several hundred wines. The restaurant is made up of three dining rooms that have each kept their authenticity, with old posters, tables set close together and a large bar near the entrance. The place is so popular that one has to be patient before being seated. Don't miss the chips, cut by hand, which are some of the best you can eat in Paris. The waiters, under pressure, waltz around the tables.

Menus / *Prix fixe menu* : 38 €.
Fermé le dimanche et le lundi / *Closed Sundays and Mondays.*

🍵 LES DÉSERTEURS
46, rue Trousseau, 75011 Paris
Métro / *Tube* : Faidherbe-Chaligny – Ledru-Rollin
+33 (0)1 48 06 95 85
www.les-deserteurs.com

Rino a cédé la place à ces Déserteurs - le chef Daniel Baratier et le sommelier Alexandre Céret - tout droit échappés de l'honorable régiment du Sergent Recruteur (4e) et de sa table plus que recommandable. L'endroit est dépouillé et microscopique, l'accueil par Alexandre met en confiance. Le menu fixe permet à Daniel de proposer une cuisine où la sobriété est au service de la justesse : produits remarquables (ah, les tomates du jardin de Marie...), heureux mariages de saveurs (quand l'anguille fumée rencontre le haricot maïs...). Ici on est surpris par une herbe inconnue, là par un produit que l'on croyait connaître... La carte des vins y est aussi intelligente que la cuisine grâce à une sélection originale et cependant raisonnée de vins français et étrangers. Une adresse petite par la taille mais grande par l'inspiration !

> *Rino has been replaced by these "Déserteurs" – the chef Daniel Baratier and the sommelier Alexandre Céret – who both deserted the honourable regiment of the Sergent Recruteur (a restaurant in the 4th arrondissement) and its highly recommended cuisine. The setting is very small and quite stark, but Alexandre's warm welcome more than makes up for it. The set menu allows Daniel to offer dishes that are both understated and remarkably well executed, with top quality produce (Ah, the tomatoes from Marie's garden...) and successful pairings (where smoked eel meets the corn bean). Occasionally, one is surprised by an unknown herb or an ingredient one thought one knew... The wine list is as intelligent as the dishes, thanks to an original but reliable selection of French and foreign wines. A place that is small in size but big on inspiration !*

Menus / *Prix fixe menu* : 28 € (déjeuner / *lunch*), 45 € (dîner / *dinner*).
Fermé le dimanche, le lundi et le mardi au déjeuner / *Closed Sundays, Mondays and Tuesdays for lunch.*

🍲 LE SERVAN

🏠 32, rue Saint-Maur, 75011 Paris
🚇 Métro / *Tube* : Père Lachaise – Rue Saint-Maur – Voltaire
+33 (0)1 55 28 51 82
www.leservan.com

Deux sœurs, l'une en salle et l'autre aux fourneaux, ont repris ce bistrot de quartier, réussissant même à lui donner un charme qu'il n'avait jamais connu depuis ses premiers débuts. La cuisine s'ouvre désormais sur la salle, un peu de couleur au mur, un éclairage plutôt soigné et autant d'attentions qui, dans le cadre d'un budget limité, permet à chacun de se sentir bien. Elles ont d'ailleurs toutes les deux le souci du détail, à l'évidence de la perfection, car le service organisé autour de deux services au dîner permet de goûter à un registre affichant un allant et une maîtrise qui forcent l'admiration. Des assiettes certes travaillées au millimètre près, mais tout autant généreuses et inspirées, avec ce qu'il faut d'assaisonnement, de texture et de croquant, de jus ou de réduction pour mettre en valeur des produits parfois canailles (cervelle, cœurs de canard) ou au contraire nobles (saint-jacques, ris de veau). Quant au paris-brest à la carte le soir de notre passage, il méritait à lui seul tous les éloges. Carte des vins pas toujours aussi convaincante, avec, bien inéluctablement, certains flacons étiquetés naturels à l'équilibre impossible.

Two sisters, one in charge of the dining room, the other in the kitchen, have taken over this neighbourhood bistro, bringing to it a charm it never had. The kitchen now opens into the dining room, the walls have been given a little colour, the lighting is carefully done and there are a lot of little things, that for a limited budget, make everyone feel good. Both sisters are clearly very attentive to detail, even perfectionists. During the two dinner sittings, one can taste admirable dishes, full of enthusiasm and savoir-faire, that are most precise in their execution but also generous and inspired, with the right amount of seasoning, texture and crunchiness, jus or reductions. They sublimate difficult ingredients (brain, duck hearts) or high-end ones (scallops, sweetbreads). As for the Paris-Brest we had for dessert, it deserves the highest praise. The wine list is not quite as convincing, with, inevitably, some natural wines with a precarious structure.

À la carte : Saint-jacques, moelle, épinards / *Scallops, bone marrow, spinach* 15 € • Mulet cru, artichaut, pomélo / *Raw hake, artichoke, pomelo* 12 € • Ris de veau, moutarde, romanesco / *Sweetbreads, mustard, romanesco* 38 € • Lieu jaune de ligne, beurre tandoori-coquillages, légumes rôtis / *Line caught Pollack, tandoori shellfish butter, roasted vegetables* 24 € • Comté, noix, salade / *Comté cheese, nuts, salad* 8 € • Paris-brest / *Paris-Brest pastry* 8 €. **Fermé le samedi, le dimanche et le lundi au déjeuner /** *Closed Saturdays, Sundays and Mondays for lunch.*

🍲 AMARANTE

🍲 4, rue Biscornet, 75012 Paris
🍲 Métro / *Tube* : Bastille – Gare de Lyon – Ledru-Rollin –
Quai de la Rapée
+33 (0)9 50 80 93 80

Christophe Philippe a quitté son restaurant du cinquième arrondissement (Chez Christophe) pour traverser la Seine. Le voilà désormais installé dans ce bistrot qui eut son heure de gloire (c'est là que Rodolphe Paquin, du Repaire de Cartouche, acquit sa notoriété), sans changer d'un poil ce qui faisait l'originalité et la réputation de son ancienne adresse : un décor rudimentaire (murs gris, banquettes rouges, miroirs), des vins nature et bio sans aucune scorie, et, l'essentiel, des produits de premier ordre, avec un goût affirmé pour les abats, apprêtés simplement de façon limpide, en droit fil de la cuisine traditionnelle. Un registre exigeant, voire élitiste, qui nous a une nouvelle fois totalement conquis.

Christophe Philippe has left his restaurant in the 5th arrondissement (Chez Christophe) and crossed the Seine. He is now settled in this once famous bistro (it's where Rodolphe Paquin from the Repaire de Cartouche first became known), without changing an iota of what made the reputation and originality of his previous venue : a rudimentary décor (grey walls, red seats, mirrors), unspoiled natural and organic wines, and most importantly first class ingredients, with a focus on offal, simply prepared in a traditional manner. A demanding, even elitist, approach, which has once again completely won us over.

Menus / *Prix fixe menu* : 19 € (déjeuner / *lunch*).
Fermé le mercredi et le jeudi / *Closed Wednesdays and Thursdays.*

🍲 WILL

🍲 75, rue Crozatier, 75012 Paris
🍲 Métro / *Tube* : Ledru-Rollin
+33 (0)1 53 17 02 44

Il a tout du bistrot contemporain, vitrine lumineuse et teintes au contraire plus sourdes à l'intérieur, mobilier vintage et accrochage minimaliste. On s'y sent d'ailleurs très bien, pas de double service au dîner qui oblige à quitter la table une fois le café avalé, et les clients trouvent souvent plaisir à prolonger le repas tard, tard dans la soirée... Ambiance réussie et cuisine enthousiasmante, jouant dans un registre plus gastronomique par les associations recherchées, la précision des techniques employées et la parfaite maîtrise des compositions. Alors bistrot gastronomique ? Oui, et pour notre plus grand plaisir car voilà l'occasion rêvée de partager en toute convivialité des assiettes tout simplement gourmandes, parfois surprenantes, mais toujours généreuses et diablement percutantes.

Will has everything that defines a contemporary bistro : large windows, toned down colours, vintage furniture and minimalist art. It is a place where one feels good. The fact that there is only one sitting for dinner means that you don't have to rush out once you've swallowed your coffee. Many clients enjoy taking their time, late into the evening...A very pleasant atmosphere and inspiring cuisine, most definitely gastronomic, with sophisticated ingredient combinations, precise techniques, and a perfect mastery of composition. So, is it a gastronomic bistro? Yes, for our greatest pleasure. Will offers the perfect opportunity to share some mouth-watering dishes, sometimes surprising, but always generous and bold.

À la carte : Gambas confites, condiment mangue/passion, écume verveine / *Slow cooked shrimp, mango/passion fruit condiment, verbena emulsion* 12 € • Tartare de bœuf, mangue verte, crème à la truffe, gomasio / *Beef tartare, green mango, truffle cream and gomasio* 12 € • Filet de cerf, mini betteraves, figues rôties, jus aigre-doux / *Venison filet, mini beetroots, roasted figs, sweet and sour jus* 24 € • Thon germon laqué, gomasio noir, zestes d'agrumes en bonbon, fenouil comme un risotto / *Albacore tuna "Peking duck" style, black gomasio, citrus zest bonbon, fennel like a risotto* 24 € • Nuage coco citron vert, glace gingembre, ananas / *Coconut lime cloud, ginger ice cream, pineapple* 9 € • Panna cotta basilic thaï, kumquats confits, sorbet yuzu / *Thai basil panna cotta, preserved kumquats, yuzu sorbet* 9 €.
Menus / *Prix fixe menu* : 45 € (dîner / *dinner*).
Fermé le dimanche et le lundi / *Closed Sundays and Mondays*.

🥮 L'AVANT-GOÛT

🍮 26, rue Bobillot, 75013 Paris
Métro / *Tube* : Place d'Italie
+33 (0)1 53 80 24 00
www.lavantgout.com

La frise de petits cochons qui cerne la salle ne doit pas aveugler : le chef aime le cochon (en pot-au-feu ou en daube) mais ne s'y cantonne pas. La carte est diverse, du foie de veau tranché épais au faisan rôti et confit, avec un goût revendiqué pour les épices (utilisées sans excès), les produits exotiques (daïkon cress, sésame noir, nouilles soba, basilic thaï, xocopili -un chocolat épicé-), les taquineries de l'acidité (rémoulade de pomme et céleri). Produit de qualité et cuissons justes. Accueil sympathique. Réservation indispensable.

The little pigs on the frieze that circles the dining room tell you that the chef loves pork (in a pot-au-feu or a daube) but not only. The menu offers interesting choices, with thick cut calf's liver, roasted and slow cooked pheasant, with a definite (but not excessive) taste for spices, exotic ingredients (daikon cress, black sesame, soba noodles, Thai basil, xocopili – a spicy chocolate), and likes to play with acidity (apple and celeriac rémoulade). Quality ingredients and precise cooking. Warm welcome. Reservations required.

Menus / *Prix fixe menu* : 33 €.
Fermé le dimanche et le lundi / *Closed Sundays and Mondays.*

🥮 L'OURCINE

🍮 92, rue Broca, 75013 Paris
Métro / *Tube* : Les Gobelins
+33 (0)1 47 07 13 65
www.restaurant-lourcine.fr

Contrat rempli pour ce bistrot qui tient toutes ses promesses. Ici rien de superflu, on va directement à l'essentiel : décor sobre, accueil et service très professionnels, rigueur de l'assiette, respect des produits.

Mission accomplished for this restaurant that keeps its promises. Nothing is superfluous, everything is straight to the point : simple décor, professional and welcoming staff, exacting dishes and ingredients treated with the utmost respect.

Menus / *Prix fixe menu* : 36 €.
Fermé le dimanche et le lundi / *Closed Sundays and Mondays.*

🍲 CETTE

🍲 7, rue Campagne Première, 75014 Paris
Métro / *Tube* : Raspail – Vavin
+33 (0)1 43 21 05 47

....

Beau comptoir en bois dans la première salle, miroirs dans la seconde, luminaires boules, murs blancs, tables en Formica impec. Même si les tables sont à touche-touche, on a une impression d'espace : elles s'alignent le long des murs, libérant le centre autour d'une desserte couverte de magnums. Il faut connaître le mode d'emploi : excellent bistro au déjeuner (et même rade de quartier avec des cafés dès 8 h du matin), remarquable resto le soir ; aux deux services, encore un chef japonais. Propositions réduites au déjeuner (2 propositions par service), carte nettement plus étoffée le soir avec des plats construits, mariant de multiples ingrédients (environ 50 €). Bons produits, variations autour du veau (carpaccio, rôti, confit, en abats...), des liquides (jus court, bouillon, velouté, consommé...), cuissons parfaites, dressages esthétiques sans chichi. Très beau choix de vins à condition de se plier à une agaçante mode qui commence à se répandre. Il n'y a aucun classement (par appellation, pays, domaine, millésime ou prix...) pour ne pas, nous dit-on « inciter les clients à se réfugier dans ce qu'ils connaissent ». Il faut donc lire ligne à ligne plusieurs pages... ou s'en remettre au patron (d'ailleurs de très bon conseil).

The handsome wood bar in the first room, the mirrors in the second, the ball shaped lights, the white walls, the formica tables, everything is just right. Even though the tables are close together, one gets a feeling of space as they are lined up against the wall, leaving the centre free for a table covered with magnums. It's important to know how this place operates : it's an excellent bistro for lunch, even a neighbourhood café open from 8 a.m., a remarkable restaurant in the evening, with two sittings, and once again a Japanese chef. The choices for lunch are limited (2 per course) but there a lot more in the evening, with structured dishes and interesting combinations of ingredients (for around 50 €). Quality products, variations on veal (carpaccio, roasted, slow cooked, offal...) and liquids (reduced jus, broth, velouté, consommé...), perfect cooking, attractive no-frills presentations. Good choice of wines, if one is willing to submit to an irritating trend that is starting to spread : there is no classification (by appellation, country, vineyard, vintage or price...). So that, as we are told, clients are more likely to stray from their comfort zone. Therefore, one has to read through several pages, line by line...or rely on the man in charge (who gives great advice).

À la carte : Velouté de patates douces, jambon fumé / *Cream of sweet potato, smoked ham* 13 € • Carpaccio de veau, herbes folles / *Veal carpaccio, "crazy" herbs* 14 € • Carré de veau, jus de cuisson, légumes / *Rack of veal, gravy, vegetables* 30 € • Turbot rôti, consommé, girolles, mousserons, choux-raves / *Roasted turbot, consommé, chanterelle mushrooms, kohlrabi* 32 € • Soufflé à la vanille / *Vanilla soufflé* 15 € • Sablé, parfait glacé, pommes, crème épaisse / *Shortbread, parfait, apples, crème fraiche* 14 €.
Menus / *Prix fixe menu* : 18 € et 22 € (déjeuner / *lunch*).
Fermé le samedi et le dimanche / *Closed Saturdays and Sundays*.

🦪 LE **CORNICHON**
🦪 34, rue Gassendi, 75014 Paris
🦪 Métro / *Tube* : Denfert-Rochereau
+33 (0)1 43 20 40 19
www.lecornichon.fr

Même quand le cucurbitacé éponyme passe à la poêle sur la carte, cet élégant bistrot (murs clairs, tables en bois, banquettes de moleskine verte, douelles peintes transformées en sculpture) ne vous prend pas pour un cornichon. La carte, réduite (quatre ou cinq propositions par service) change fréquemment. Goût affirmé pour les légumes, les produits souvent originaux (sabre), les modes de préparation variés (fricassé, croustillant, gratin, mijotage, crémeux, grillé, confit, frit...), les plats très construits. En saison, nombreux gibiers (grouse, cerf, colvert, perdrix rouge et grise, garenne, chevreuil, lièvre, sanglier, palombe, biche, faisan...) On peut s'inscrire pour être alerté de la mise sur carte de chaque gibier. Belle carte des vins (mais servis trop froids). Excellent café du torréfacteur italien Quarta et très bon pain de chez Saibron. Accueil sympathique et service rapide.

Even when the eponymous ingredient is present on the menu, this elegant bistro with its light coloured walls, wooden tables, green moleskin seats, and painted staves made into sculptures, won't put you in a pickle. The short menu (4 or 5 dishes) changes often. It shows a marked taste for vegetables, original ingredients (scabbardfish), a variety of preparations (fricassee, crisped, au gratin, slow cooked, creamy, grilled, preserved, fried...), very structured dishes, a lot of venison in season (grouse, deer, mallard, red and grey partridge, wild rabbit, hare, boar, wood pigeon, pheasant...). You can sign up to be alerted when a particular type of venison gets put on the menu. Good wine list (but served too cold). Excellent coffee from the Italian Roaster Quarta and very good bread from Saibron. Warm welcome and efficient service.

À la carte : Velouté de pommes de terre, haddock fumé, purée de persil et petits croûtons / *Potato velouté, smoked haddock, parsley purée, croutons* 12 € • Moules frites, retour d'Étretat / *Mussels and chips, Etretat style* 12 € • Râgout de haricots de Paimpol aux supions grillés, sauge, tomates et persil / *Paimpol beans ragout with grilled squid, sage, tomatoes and parsley* 22 € • Palombe cuisinée en croûte de sel, lentilles vertes du Puy mijotées au lard / *Wood pigeon cooked in a salt crust, green lentils from the Puy cooked with bacon* 32 € • Camembert au lait cru de Normandie / *Raw milk Camembert from Normandy* 9 € • Figues pochées aux épices, sorbet faisselle de chèvre, crumble de noix et pointes de praliné / *Poached figs with spices, goat milk sorbet, nut crumble and praline bits* 9 €.
Menus / *Prix fixe menu* : 35 € (déjeuner / *lunch*, dîner / *dinner*, semaine / *week*).
Fermé le samedi et le dimanche / *Closed Saturdays and Sundays*.

🍲 LES PETITES SORCIÈRES
🍲 12, rue Liancourt, 75014 Paris
🍲 Métro / *Tube* : Denfert-Rochereau
+33 (0)1 43 21 95 68

Entre l'imbattable menu du déjeuner (25 €) et celui nettement plus onéreux du dîner (59 €), une cuisine toujours aussi passionnante et exemplaire. La différence de prix s'explique parfaitement par le choix des ingrédients et des morceaux à l'évidence plus nobles le soir. Cette précision apportée, avouons d'emblée que nous avons le même plaisir à retrouver les deux registres et qu'il est possible ici de faire deux repas dans la même journée sans pour autant ressasser les mêmes plats (ni donc les mêmes ingrédients...). Et, de plus en plus rares à Paris, les poissons sont ici d'une rare qualité (c'en est presque la spécialité) et les desserts sont uniques car emprunts d'une douce nostalgie enfantine.

Whether it's the unbeatable lunch menu (25 €) or the much more expensive one for dinner (59 €), the cuisine is always as exciting and exemplary. The price difference is totally justified by the choice of ingredients, which are much more "high-end" in the evening. Now that that's out of the way, we have to say that we enjoy both, and that it is possible to enjoy two meals here in the same day without the dishes (or the ingredients) being repetitive. And, as is less and less frequent in Paris, the fish is of a very high standard (it's almost a speciality) and the desserts are unique in the childhood nostalgia that they bring to the table.

Menus / *Prix fixe menu* : 25 € (déjeuner / *lunch*), 59 € (dîner / *dinner*).
Fermé le dimanche et le lundi / *Closed Sundays and Mondays.*

🍲 LE GRAND PAN

🍲 20, rue Rosenwald, 75015 Paris
🍲 Métro / *Tube* : Convention – Plaisance
+33 (0)1 42 50 02 50
www.legrandpan.fr

« Aujourd'hui ça et là, les gens boivent encore, et le feu du nectar fait toujours luire les trognes... » écrivait le bon Georges. On n'est pas si loin, rue Rozenwald, de l'impasse Florimont où Brassens écrivit Le grand Pan, qui donne son nom à ce bistrot d'angle, généreux et bonhomme. Benoît Gauthier passé par des maisons qui engagent à la gourmandise et à la fraternité (Dutournier, Etchebest...), propose une cuisine solide mais élégante : des côtes de bœuf et de veau dodues et juteuses, des frites au couteau brûle-doigts, des desserts classiques - mont-blanc, far aux pruneaux... - mais réjouissants. Brassens craignait que « la fin du monde ne soit bien triste »... Elle épargnera Le grand Pan, mais aussi Le petit Pan, l'annexe d'en face qui propose une cuisine plus simple, mais armée des mêmes intentions...

We're not far in the rue Rosenwald, from the impasse Florimond, where the famous George Brassens, wrote his song : Le Grand Pan, which gave its name to this generous and cheerful bistro. Benoit Gauthier who has worked in restaurants which promote very good food and friendship (Dutournier, Etchebest...) serves up a cuisine that is both reliable and elegant : beef and veal rib steaks that are plump and juicy, hand cut chips to be eaten by hand and classical but comforting desserts : Mont-Blanc, prune flan...Brassens was worried that "The end of the world be quite sad...". The Grand Pan as well as the Petit Pan, its annex, which offers simpler dishes, prepared in the same spirit, will no doubt be spared...

À la carte : Soupe crémeuse de légumes oubliés, noisettes et brunoise de chorizo / *Creamy soup of heirloom vegetables, hazelnuts and chopped chorizo* 8 € • Épaule d'agneau braisée longuement, haricots coco / *Slow cooked shoulder of lamb, "coco" beans* 14 € • Pavé de merlu à la plancha / *Hake filet "à la plancha"* 14 € • Mont-blanc façon Grand Pan / *Mont-Blanc Gran Pan style* 7 € • Verrine au chocolat dulcey et mousse chocolat jivara / *Verrine of dulcey chocolate and jivara chocolate mousse* 7 €.
Menus / *Prix fixe menu* : 21 € (déjeuner / *lunch*).
Fermé le samedi et le dimanche / *Closed Saturdays and Sundays.*

JADIS

208, rue de la Croix-Nivert, 75015 Paris
Métro / *Tube* : Boucicaut – Convention
+33 (0)1 45 57 73 20
www.bistrotjadisparis.com

Dans un décor reposant et sans prétention, vous serez accueillis et servis avec le sourire, et dégusterez les superbes préparations « bistronomiques » du chef Guillaume Delage : des plats traditionnels revus et corrigés avec une invention sans faille, accompagnés de vins délicieux. Vous l'avez compris, une adresse incontournable du Paris des bons vivants.

In this unpretentious and soothing setting, you will be welcomed and served with a smile, and you will get to taste some superb "bistronomic" fare by the chef Guillaume Delage : traditional dishes creatively reinvented, accompanied by delicious wines. It's one of the "places to be" in Paris for food lovers, that you shouldn't miss out on.

Menus / *Prix fixe menu* : 26 € (déjeuner / *lunch*), 36 € (dîner / *dinner*).
Fermé le samedi et le dimanche / *Closed Saturdays and Sundays.*

🍲 ATELIER VIVANDA

🍲 18, rue Lauriston, 75016 Paris
🍲 Métro / *Tube* : Charles-de-Gaulle Étoile
+33 (0)1 40 67 10 00
www.ateliervivanda.fr

On aime bien l'aménagement avec ses tables et ses peaux qui recouvrent les banquettes, le vis-à-vis des fourneaux qui permet de suivre la cuisson des préparations. On aime beaucoup l'engagement du chef Akrame Benallal qui sait se remettre ici en question pour proposer une carte des plus simples - viandes et pommes de terre - mais exécutée à la perfection. Desserts tout aussi réussis dans un registre ménager et carte des vins d'une grande intelligence. Tarifs restés raisonnables.

We like the way this place is set up, with its tables, pelts covering the seats, and the view of the kitchen that allows one to watch the food being cooked. We love the commitment of chef Akrame Benallal who doesn't hesitate to challenge himself by offering the simplest of menus - meat and potatoes - perfectly executed. The home style desserts are just as convincing and the wine selection is spot on. The prices are reasonable.

Menus / *Prix fixe menu* : 35 €.
Fermé le samedi et le dimanche / *Closed Saturdays and Sundays.*

🥟 LE 975

🥟 25, rue Guy Môquet, 75017 Paris
Métro / *Tube* : Brochant – Guy Môquet
+33 (0)9 53 75 67 71
www.le975.com

Immanquable, ce récent bistrot l'est de façon incontestable... Imaginez une sorte de container d'angle, boisé et vitré, aux montants jaune citron, avec cuisine comptoir (et deux officiants nippons) et les désormais incontournables chaises d'école réformées et pierres grattées. Tout l'attirail des adresses un brin modeuses, mais ici parfaitement fiable grâce à des assiettes aux ingrédients nettement définis, aux assaisonnements justes et sans emprunt aux tics du moment, même si l'on retrouve quelques gadgets ici et là (oeuf parfait, burrata...). Service attentif (quoique le déroulé du repas soit un peu long) et jolie carte des vins tendance bio-nature.

This recent bistro is most definitely a "place to be"... Imagine a sort of wooden container, with glass windows and bright yellow trimmings, a countertop/kitchen (and two Japanese cooks) and the often seen, revamped school chairs and scraped stonework. It has everything required to make it a trendy venue, but it is worth trying out. The dishes are prepared with well defined ingredients, precise seasonings, without all the current mannerisms, even if some "gadgets" can be found here or there (perfect egg, burrata...). The staff are attentive (but the meal takes a little too long). Nice wine list with a focus on fashionable organic/natural wines.

À la carte : Tataki de saumon écossais Label Rouge, miso blanc et vinaigrette aux agrumes / *Scottish « Label Rouge » salmon tataki, white miso and citrus vinaigrette 12 €* • Œuf parfait, magret fumé, girolles et amandes / *Perfect egg, smoked duck breast, chanterelle mushrooms and almonds 14 €* • Selle d'agneau du Cantal au romarin, citron confit, caviar d'aubergines et légumes / *Saddle of lamb from the Cantal, with rosemary, preserved lemon, eggplant caviar, and vegetables 28 €* • Dos de cabillaud du Guilvinec sauce vierge, salade de légumes verts croquants / *Cod filet from the Guilvinec, « vierge » sauce, crisp green vegetable salad 23 €* • Blanc-manger au thé jasmin, mangue et gelée coco / *Jasmine tea blancmange, mango and coconut jelly 9 €.*
Fermé le samedi midi et le dimanche toute la journée / *Closed Saturdays for lunch and Sundays.*

🍲 GARE AU GORILLE
🍲 68, rue des Dames, 75017 Paris
🍲 Métro / *Tube* : Place de Clichy – Rome
   +33 (0)1 42 94 24 02

On aime beaucoup la cuisine fondue et intelligente qui met en avant les produits sans les juxtaposer, millimétrée, très pensée et même sexy. La carte des vins est bien achalandée avec certains flacons « venus d'ailleurs » (Grèce et Italie notamment) que l'on ne trouve pas sur toutes les tables. Au dîner, il est possible de partager entre amis des plats « façon tapas » tout aussi enthousiasmants. Service compétent, sympathique et convivialité garantie. Une vraie réussite !

We really enjoyed this intelligent cuisine, which highlights ingredients without juxtaposing them. It's meticulous, thought-out and even sexy. The wine list is well chosen with some "foreign" bottles (Greek and Italian mostly) that you won't find everywhere. For dinner, you can share "tapas style" dishes that are just as inspiring. The staff are competent and friendly. A good time is guaranteed. A real success !

À la carte : Coques, poivron, chorizo / *Clams, bell pepper, chorizo* 9 € • Bœuf cru, oursin, chou-fleur / *Raw beef, urchin, cauliflower* 14 € • Agneau, harissa, sauce blanche / *Lamb, harissa, white sauce* 9 € • Rouget en escabèche, fenouil, orange / *Red mullet "escabèche", fennel, orange* 12 € • Tarte citron, pomelos, meringue / *Lemon tart, pomelo, meringue* 8 €.
Fermé le dimanche et le lundi / *Closed Sundays and Mondays*.

🍲 LES GRANDES BOUCHES
🍲 78, rue de Lévis, 75017 Paris
🍲 Métro / *Tube* : Malesherbes
   +33 (0)1 43 80 40 36
   www.lesgrandesbouches.com

Pierres grattées, grands miroirs, table en bois, banquettes confortables : ces Grandes Bouches ont de la gueule et une carte ramassée (deux propositions par service). Non seulement les assiettes sont esthétiquement dressées et colorées, mais leur contenu est souvent original dans la

recherche des produits (criste marine, champignon spa-
rassis crépu) ou les associations de saveurs, avec des clins
d'œil orientaux maîtrisés. Régulièrement, des semaines ou
soirées à thème (tout tomates, gibier, abats, locavores...).
Les viandes maturées deux mois sont servies saignantes.
Bon choix de vins, souvent originaux. Service particulière-
ment attentif.

*Pale stonework, large mirrors, wooden tables, comfortable
seats, these "Grandes Bouches" have a lot to say for them-
selves and a short menu (two choices per course). Not only
are the dishes colourful and attractively presented, but the
choice of ingredients is also original (criste marine, cauli-
flower mushrooms) as are the flavour combinations, and
the light oriental touches. They offer weeklong or evening
themes (100% tomato, venison, offal, locavore...). The
meat is aged for two months and served rare. Good wine list
with original selections. The service is especially attentive.*

Menus / *Prix fixe menu* : 32 € (déjeuner / *lunch*), 40 € (dîner /
dinner).
**Fermé le samedi au déjeuner, le dimanche et le lundi toute la
journée /** *Closed Saturdays for lunch, Sundays and Mondays.*

🍲 L'ESQUISSE
🍲 151 bis, rue Marcadet, 75018 Paris
Métro / *Tube* : Lamarck-Caulaincourt
+33 (0)1 53 41 63 04

Banquette de métro et fauteuils métalliques sur fond brun, façade réduite qui laisse place à une salle de plus grande ampleur avec cuisine ouverte où officie peinardement une jeune femme, Laetitia, ex du Bistral, et qui est passée aussi par le Ritz... Telle se présente cette sympathique maison où le service est assuré par Thomas, calé en vins tendance nature (Pithon, Guillot-Broux, Lapalu, Sernin Berrux...), et garantissant un « deux font la paire » efficace ! L'ardoise du jour est séductrice, reposant sur des bases classiques, toujours relancées par des légumes intéressants, des épices et des condiments, de caractère contemporain.

Metro seats and metal chairs on a brown background, a small façade that leads to a larger dining room with an open kitchen, where a young woman, Laetitia, who worked at the Bistral and at the Ritz, cooks quite peacefully. This is what to expect in this friendly restaurant, where Thomas, who is quite knowledgeable about natural wines (Pithon, Guillot-Broux, Lapalu, Sernin Berrux...), is in charge of the service, making for an efficient duo. The daily menu is attractive, with traditional dishes, made more exciting with interesting, contemporary, vegetables, spices and condiments.

À la carte : Panna cotta au chèvre, betteraves collection / *Goat cheese panna cotta, heirloom beetroots* 7 € • Ravioles de boudin noir, consommé de pommes de terre / *Black pudding ravioli, potato consommé* 9 € • Poitrine de veau braisée, coques, câpres, julienne de poireaux / *Braised veal breast, cockles, capers, leek julienne* 20 € • Saint-jacques poêlées, topinambour, gingembre, émulsion café / *Pan fried scallops, Jerusalem artichoke, ginger, coffee emulsion* 20 € • Pressé de coings-agrumes, glace miel-bergamote / *Quince citrus terrine, bergamot honey ice cream* 8 € • Tarte briochée aux pralines roses de Lyon / *Brioche style tart with pink pralines from Lyon* 7 €.
Menus / *Prix fixe menu* : 22 € (déjeuner / *lunch*).
Fermé le dimanche et le lundi / *Closed Sundays and Mondays.*

🍲 MIROIR

🍲 94, rue des Martyrs, 75018 Paris
Métro / *Tube* : Abbesses
+33 (0)1 46 06 50 73
www.restaurantmiroir.com

Dans cette maison des Abbesses, Sébastien Guenard fait une cuisine à son image : ronde et joyeuse. Les saisons l'inspirent et il se surpasse à l'automne quand le gibier est à sa carte. Son savoir-faire reste large comme en attestent son foie gras en entrée ou sa quenelle de chocolat en dessert. Quant à la cave, elle vaut tout simplement le détour... quitte à traverser la rue après le repas pour acheter les bouteilles dégustées. Délicieux pain de Thierry Breton à la croûte épaisse. Service à la fois dynamique et sympathique.

In this Abbesses restaurant, Sébastien Guénard, prepares food that resembles him : well-rounded and cheerful. The seasons inspire him and particularly autumn when he surpasses himself with the venison on his menu. He offers a wide range of skilfully prepared dishes, from foie gras for starters to chocolate quenelle for dessert. The cellar is definitely worth the trip... You can even cross the road after your meal to buy the bottles you enjoyed. Delicious bread from Thierry Breton with a nice thick crust. The service is both lively and friendly.

À la carte : Terrine de biche aux foies, champignons / *Venison liver terrine, mushrooms* 12 € • Salade de pommes de terre et langue de bœuf / *Potato salad and beef tongue* 12 € • Épaule braisée, aubergines, poivrons / *Braised shoulder, eggplants, bell peppers* 22 € • Pavé de dorade snacké, carottes / *Grilled bream fillet, carrots* 22 € • Tarte amandine aux poires / *Amandine pear tart* 11 € • Salade de fruits exotiques glacée, chantilly mangue / *Exotic iced fruit salad, mango whipped cream* 11 €.
Menus / *Prix fixe menu* : 34 € (déjeuner / *lunch*), 44 € (dîner / *dinner*).
Fermé le dimanche et le lundi / *Closed Sundays and Mondays*.

🍲 LA RALLONGE

🍲 16, rue Eugène Sue, 75018 Paris
🍲 Métro / *Tube* : Jules Joffrin – Marcadet-Poissonniers
+33 (0)1 42 59 43 24
www.larallonge.fr

Au pied de la butte Montmartre, ce bistrot mérite infiniment mieux que l'appellation d'annexe, même si la Table d'Eugène sise à quelques mètres en est la maison mère. La salle, le comptoir et ses hauts tabourets rappellent les meilleurs bars à tapas espagnols, tout comme la cuisine inspirée de Geoffroy Maillard et du chef de cuisine Damien Le Bozec : tapas et pinchos néo-basques de haute volée, qui nous transportent au-delà des Pyrénées (chipirons, croquettes de Serrano, pain à la catalane, etc.). Jolie sélection de flacons par Virginie Gomez, la sommelière avisée. Service ibérique, aussi efficace que chaleureux.

At the foot of the Butte Montmartre, this bistro deserves to be recognized as more than an annex, even if the Table d'Eugène a few meters away is its "parent" restaurant. The dining room, the bar and the high stools are all reminiscent of the best Spanish tapas bars, as is the inspired cuisine of Geoffroy Maillard and of chef Damien Le Bozec : high flying neo-Basque tapas and pinchos that transport you over the Pyrenees (baby squid, Serrano ham croquettes, pan catalan, etc.). Nice selection of bottles by Virginie Gomez, the savvy sommelier. Iberian service, efficient and friendly.

À la carte : Mousseline de panais, chocolat blanc et chips de légumes / *Parsnip mousse, white chocolate and vegetable crisps* 7 € • Couteaux à la plancha, huile vierge de saison / *Razorclams « à la plancha », seasonal virgin oil* 10 € • Pigeon en deux cuissons, cuisse à la plancha, abattis en croustillant, mousseline de betteraves / *Pigeon cooked two ways, leg « à la pancha », giblet "croustillant", beetroot mousse* 8 € • Saint-jacques snackées, condiments de légumes à la thaïe, nuage de saté / *Grilled scallops, Thai vegetable condiment, cloud of satay* 10 € • Chantilly chocolat au lait / *Milk chocolate Chantilly* 6 € • Litchi, sspuma yaourt à la rose, confiture de fruits rouges, sésame / *Litchi, rose yogurt emulsion, red berry jam* 6,50 €.
Fermé le dimanche et le lundi / *Closed Sundays and Mondays.*

🍽 LE BARATIN

🍲 3, rue Jouye-Rouve, 75020 Paris
Métro / *Tube* : Belleville – Pyrénées
+33 (0)1 43 49 39 70

Ce serait presque un bistrot à la Doisneau, posé dans un quartier populaire, sans fioriture, avec sa clientèle d'habitués-connaisseurs, voire de vignerons de passage, qui se regroupent au comptoir autour d'une vingtaine de vins au verre, toujours remarquablement chinés par « Pinuche », l'homme du tire-bouchon. Une vraie gueule d'atmosphère, non frelatée, à laquelle Raquel donne tout son sel en cuisine, absolument inimitable dans son genre, car faite avec amour, comme seules les « mamans » savent la délivrer (elle rend également un hommage régulier aux abats, cervelle et ris de veau, etc.). Pour plus de libations bacchiques, voir Pinuche et sa cave (communiquée de bouche à oreille) qui recèle quelques 300 références. Excellent menu déjeuner.

There's a definite Doisneau ambiance to this no frills bistro, in its unpretentious neighbourhood, with its clientele of regulars/connoisseurs, or even of winemakers who just happen to be in the area, all gathered around the bar to taste some of the 20 or so, wines by the glass, remarkably selected by "Pinuche" the man with the corkscrew. An authentic atmosphere, to which Raquel brings her special inimitable touch in the kitchen, where everything is made with love, as only "mothers" can do. She is also a big fan of offal (brains, sweetbreads, etc.). For more bacchic libations, you need to see Pinuche and his cellar, which holds over 300 wines. Excellent lunch menu.

À la carte : Artichauts poivrade, ragoût citron / *Poivrade artichokes, lemon ragout* 11 € • Carpaccio de bar de ligne / *Line caught sea bass carpaccio* 13 € • Joues de bœuf croustillantes aux légumes / *Crispy beef cheeks with vegetables* 20 € • Tripes et pied de veau en ragoût / *Offal and veal trotter ragout* 26 € • Fondant au chocolat / *Chocolate fondant* 8 € • Tartelette au fromage blanc et fruits/ *Cream cheese and fruit tartlet* 8 €.
Menus / *Prix fixe menu* : 19 € (déjeuner / *lunch*, semaine / *week*). **Fermé le samedi midi, le dimanche et le lundi /** *Closed Saturdays for lunch, Sundays and Mondays.*

🥟 DILIA

🥟 1 rue d'Eupatoria, 75020 Paris
Métro / *Tube* : Ménilmontant
+33 (0)9 53 56 24 14
www.dilia.fr

Entre Belleville et Ménilmontant, un lieu à la mode et bobo. Mais la cuisine du toscan Michele Farnesi, qui œuvre seul, ramène vite l'attention aux fondamentaux. C'est beau, c'est bon, précis dans les cuissons et étonnant dans certaines associations de produits sélectionnés avec brio.

Between Belleville and Menilmontant, a bohemian district to be seen in. But the cuisine of the Tuscan Chef Michele Farnesi who is alone at the helm, is enough to grab one's attention. It's beautiful, it's tasty, executed with precision, and some of the combinations of well-chosen ingredients can be surprising.

Menus / *Prix fixe menu* : 45 € (déjeuner / *lunch)*, 70 € (dîner / *dinner)*.
Fermé le dimanche et le lundi / *Closed Sundays and Mondays.*

PARIS

51 autres bonnes adresses /
51 *other good addresses*

1er arrondissement

RACINES 2
39, rue de l'Arbre Sec – 75001
Métro / *Tube* : Louvre – Rivoli
+33 (0)1 42 60 77 34

ZÉBULON
10, rue de Richelieu – 75001
Métro / *Tube* : Palais Royal – Musée du Louvre
+33 (0)1 42 36 49 44

2e arrondissement

CHEZ GEORGES - LE JEU DU MAIL
1, rue du Mail – 75002
Métro / *Tube* : Bourse – Sentier
+33 (0)1 42 60 0711

4e arrondissement

BENOIT
20, rue Saint-Martin – 75004
Métro / *Tube* : Châtelet – Hôtel de Ville
+33 (0)1 42 72 25 76

5e arrondissement

PAPILLES
30, rue Gay-Lussac – 75005
Métro / *Tube* : Cardinal Lemoine
+33 (0)1 43 25 20 79

VIN SOBRE
25, rue des Feuillantines – 75005
Métro / *Tube* : Censier - Daubenton
+33 (0)1 43 29 00 23

6e arrondissement

RESTAURANT AUX PRÉS
27, rue du Dragon – 75006
Métro / *Tube* : Saint-Germain-des-Prés
+33 (0)1 45 48 29 68

COMPTOIR DU RELAIS
9, carrefour de l'Odéon – 75006
Métro / *Tube* : Odéon
+33 (0)1 44 27 07 97

H KITCHEN
18, rue Mayet Paris – 75006
Métro / *Tube* : Duroc – Falguière – Vaneau
+33 (0)1 45 66 51 57

SEMILLA
54, rue de Seine– 75006
Métro / *Tube* : Saint-Germain-des-Prés
+33 (0)1 43 54 34 50

7ᵉ arrondissement

AMI JEAN
27, rue Malar – 75007
Métro / *Tube* : Invalides – La Tour-Maubourg
+33 (0)1 47 05 86 89

CAFÉ CONSTANT
139, rue Saint-Dominique – 75007
Métro / *Tube* : École Militaire
+33 (0)1 47 53 73 34

POTTOKA
4, rue de l'Exposition – 75007
Métro / *Tube* : École Militaire
+33 (0)1 45 51 88 38

8ᵉ arrondissement

LAZARE
Parvis de la gare Saint-Lazare – 75008
Métro / *Tube* : Saint-Lazare
+33 (0)1 44 90 80 80

MONSIEUR
11, rue du Cheval de Saint-George – 75008
Métro / *Tube* : Madeleine
+33 (0)1 42 60 14 36

RENOMA GALLERY
32, avenue George V – 75008
Métro / *Tube* : Alma Marceau – George V
+33 (0)1 47 20 46 19

9e arrondissement

AFFRANCHIS
5, rue Henri Monnier – 75009
Métro / *Tube* : Pigalle – Saint-Georges
+33 (0)1 45 26 26 30

BISTROT LA BRUYÈRE
31, rue Labruyère – 75009
Métro / *Tube* : Saint-Georges
+33 (0)9 81 22 20 56

CANAILLES
25, rue de Labruyère – 75009
Métro / *Tube* : Saint-Georges
+33 (0)1 48 74 10 48

DIABLES AU THYM
35, rue Bergère – 75009
Métro / *Tube* : Grands Boulevards
+33 (0)1 47 70 77 09

10e arrondissement

52 FAUBOURG SAINT-DENIS
52, rue du Faubourg Saint-Denis – 75010
Métro / *Tube* : Château d'Eau
+33 (0)

BISTROT BELLET
84, rue du Faubourg-Saint-Denis – 75010
Métro / *Tube* : Château d'Eau
+33 (0)1 45 23 42 06

GALOPIN
34, rue Saint-Marthe – 75010
Métro / *Tube* : Colonel Fabien
+33 (0)1 42 06 05 03

PARADIS
14, rue de Paradis – 75010
Métro / *Tube* : Château d'Eau – Gare de l'Est
+33 (0)1 45 23 57 98

VERRE VOLÉ
67, rue de Lancry – 75010
Métro / *Tube* : Gare de l'Est – Jacques Bonsergent
+33 (0)1 48 03 17 34

11e arrondissement

6, PAUL BERT
6, rue Paul Bert – 75011
Métro / *Tube* : Charonne – Faidherbe-Chaligny –
Rue des Boulets
+33 (0)1 43 79 14 32

CLOWN BAR
114, rue Amelot – 75011
Métro / *Tube* : Filles du Calvaire – Oberkampf
+33 (0)1 43 55 87 35

PULPERIA
11, rue Richard Lenoir – 75011
Métro / *Tube* : Charonne
+33 (0)1 40 09 03 70

REPAIRE DE CARTOUCHE
8, boulevard des Filles-du-Calvaire – 75011
Métro / *Tube* : Saint-Sébastien-Froissart
+33 (0)1 47 00 25 86

VILLARET
13, rue Ternaux – 75011
Métro / *Tube* : Oberkampf – Parmentier
+33 (0)1 43 57 89 76

12ᵉ arrondissement

AUBERGE LE QUINCY
28, avenue Ledru-Rollin – 75012
Métro / *Tube* : Gare de Lyon – Quai de la Rapée
+33 (0)1 46 28 46 76

14ᵉ arrondissement

CERISAIE
70, boulevard Edgar-Quinet – 75014
Métro / *Tube* : Edgar Quinet – Montparnasse-Bienvenue
+33 (0)1 43 20 98 98

🍲 ESSENTIEL
🍲 168, rue d'Alésia – 75014
Métro / *Tube* : Alésia
+33 (0)1 45 42 64 80

🍲 GRANDE OURSE
🍲 9, rue Georges-Saché – 75014
Métro / *Tube* : Alésia – Mouton-Duvernet – Pernety
+33 (0)1 40 44 67 85

🍲 NINA
🍲 139, rue du Château – 75014
Métro / *Tube* : Pernety – Gaîté
+33 (0)9 83 01 88 40

🍲 PETITS PLATS
🍲 39, rue des Plantes – 75014
Métro / *Tube* : Alésia
+33 (0)1 45 42 50 52

🍲 RÉGALADE
🍲 49, avenue Jean-Moulin – 75014
Métro / *Tube* : Alésia – Porte d'Orléans
+33 (0)1 45 45 68 58

15e arrondissement

🍲 AFARIA
🍲 15, rue Desnouettes – 75015
Métro / *Tube* : Convention
+33 (0)1 48 42 95 90

BEURRE NOISETTE
68, rue Vasco-de-Gama – 75015
Métro / *Tube* : Lourmel – Porte de Versailles
+33 (0)1 48 56 82 49

CASSENOIX
56, rue de la Fédération – 75015
Métro / *Tube* : Bir-Hakeim – Dupleix
+33 (0)1 45 66 09 01

LE 41 PASTEUR
41, boulevard Pasteur – 75015
Métro / *Tube* : Pasteur
+33 (0)1 47 34 15 50

16ᵉ arrondissement

GÉRAUD
31, rue Vital – 75016
Métro / *Tube* : La Muette
+33 (0)1 45 20 33 00

17ᵉ arrondissement

CAVES PÉTRISSANS
30 bis, avenue Niel – 75017
Métro / *Tube* : Charles de Gaulle-Étoile – Pereire – Ternes
+33 (0)1 42 27 52 03

ENTREDGEU
83, rue Laugier – 75017
Métro / *Tube* : Porte de Champerret
+33 (0)1 40 54 97 24

⚬ GOUPIL LE BISTROT
4, rue Claude-Debussy – 75017
Métro / *Tube* : Porte de Champerret
+33 (0)1 45 74 83 25

⚬ POULETTES BATIGNOLLES
10, rue de Chéroy – 75017
Métro / *Tube* : Rome
+33 (0)1 42 93 10 11

⚬ ROCA
31, rue Guillaume Tell – 75017
Métro / *Tube* : Pereire
+33 (0)1 47 64 86 04

⚬ XVII SUR VIN
99, rue Jouffroy d'Abbans – 75017
Métro / *Tube* : Wagram
+33 (0)1 42 27 26 16

18ᵉ arrondissement

⚬ COQ RICO
98, rue Lepic – 75018
Métro / *Tube* : Abbesses
+33 (0)1 42 59 82 89

⚬ NOMOS
15, rue André del Sarte – 75018
Métro / *Tube* : Anvers – Château rouge –
Barbès Rochechouart
+33 (0)6 95 84 75 97

20ᵉ arrondissement

☕ CHATOMAT
6, rue Victor-Letalle – 75020
Métro / *Tube* : Ménilmontant
+33 (0)1 47 97 25 77

LONDON

North London

🍽 THE ALBION

🍽 10 Thornhill Road, Islington, London N1 1HW
🍽 Tube / *Métro* : Angel (Northern Line)
  + 44 207 607 7450
  www.the-albion.co.uk

....

The Albion is a Georgian Inn dating back to the time when Londoners would escape the summer heat and dirt by walking to the rural idyll of Islington. Times change, and while the capital has long since swallowed the area, the walled garden of the Albion is still an oasis for local residents and worker on sunny days – or indeed any day when it's not actually too wet or cold to sit to sit out. The main menu, with a focus on fresh, seasonal produce, is supplemented by a summer barbecue, although alfresco diners should check that it's running. Portions tend to be on the generous side, so anyone looking for a light lunch should browse the small plate menu. At the other end of the scale, delicious Whole Roast Sucking Pig with all the trimmings is a house speciality, requiring 72 hours' notice and feeding 10 to 15 diners for £400.

Une auberge qui date de l'époque géorgienne, quand les Londoniens aimaient se promener dans ce coin champêtre d'Islington pour échapper à la chaleur ou poussière de l'été... Quelques siècles plus tard, l'Albion est toujours là, avec son jardin ombragé, abrité derrière les murs, si agréable pour déguster dès les beaux jours des grillades préparées devant vous sur le barbecue. Les portions se montrent généreuses et la carte des "petites assiettes" parfaite pour déjeuner léger. Bon à savoir, le cochon de lait entier servi accompagné de nombreuses garnitures est la

74

spécialité de la maison et régale jusqu'à quinze personnes (à commander 72 heures à l'avance et compter environ 400 £ pour le groupe).

À la carte : Brixham crab, green apple and mascarpone, thyme croûtons / *Crabe de Brixham, pomme granny et mascarpone, croûtons au thym* 8,50 £ • Slow roast smoked pork shoulder and trotters, butter beans, toast / *Épaule et pieds de porc confits, haricots beurre* 8,50 £ • 28 day aged Longhorn rib eye on the bone 350g / *Faux-filet sur l'os, maturé 28 jours* 21,50 £ • Sussex barnsley chop / *Côte filet double d'agneau du Sussex* 15,50 £ • Pan fried sea trout, grilled fennel, saffron cream / *Truite poêlée, fenouil grillé, crème au safran* 16,50 £ • Rhubarb and gooseberry fool, gingernut biscuits / *Fool rhubarbe et groseille à maquereau, biscuits à la noix et au gingembre* 6,50 £.
Open every day / *Ouvert tous les jours*

🍺 THE BULL
🍲 13 North Hill, Highgate N6 4AB
Tube / *Métro* : Highgate (Northern Line)
+ 44 20 8341 0510
www.thebullhighgate.co.uk

It's well worth the walk up the hill from Highgate village towards Hampstead Heath to enjoy one of London's best brewpubs. The Bull is an imposing inn that has been updated to combine owner Dan Fox's passion for beer with an interesting gastropub menu built around local and seasonal produce. Beer and food matching is a speciality of the Bull, and so all dishes come with a recommended beer or cider accompaniment, either brewed at the pub or from the extensive range of British and imported beer available. For those who prefer, the wine list is also well worth exploring. Along with a full restaurant menu, the tempting traditional home- made bar snacks such as the Bull's sausage roll or pickled gherkins accompanied by a pint of cask ale are just the job after a brisk walk.

Il ne faut pas hésiter à grimper la côte du village de Highgate pour se rendre à Hampstead Heath car vous y trouverez l'un des meilleurs pubs-microbrasseries de Londres. Cette adresse n'a pas eu de mal à s'imposer en associant à la passion pour la bière de son propriétaire, Dan Fox, une carte riche en produits locaux et de saison.

Aussi, les associations bières et mets font la réputation de la maison, tous les plats étant proposés accompagnés d'une mousse, qu'elle soit brassée ici ou issue de sélection de marques britanniques ou importées. Que ceux qui préfèrent le vin se rassurent, la cave mérite tout autant le détour... À côté de la carte, il est possible de se sustenter d'en-cas également faits maison, comme le sandwich à la saucisse ou les cornichons, qui, accompagnés d'une pinte, sont tout aussi mérités après un bonne balade dans le quartier...

À la carte : Chicken, parma ham and leek terrine, piccalilli and toast / *Terrine de poulet, jambon de Parme et poireaux, condiment piccalilli et toast* 8,50 £ • Confit duck, waffle, male and chilli glaze / *Confit de canard laqué au piment et à l'hydromel, gaufre* 7,50 £ • Hampshire pork chop, Jersey royals, edamame beans, broccoli stalks, chilli, fire and brimstone sauce / *Côte de porc du Hampshire, pommes de terre Jersey Royal, haricots edamame, tiges de brocoli, sauce au piment* 12,50 £ • 28 day Dexter rump steak, garlic butter, homemade chips, watercress / *Rumstek de Dexter maturé 28 jours, beurre d'ail, frites maison, cresson* 16,50 £ • Beer battered sustainable haddock and chips, minted mushy peas, tartar sauce, lemon / *Haddock de pêche durable pané à la bière, frites, écrasée de petits pois à la menthe, sauce tartare* 11,95 £.
Open every day / *Ouvert tous les jours*

🥧 THE BULL & LAST

🥧 168 Highgate Road, London NW5 1QS
🥧 Tube / *Métro* : Tufnell Park (Northern)
+44 20 7267 3641
www.thebullandlast.co.uk

After a long period in the gastronomic wilderness for British bar snacks, there has been a movement amongst chefs to reinvent and rehabilitate the likes of pork pies and scratchings over recent years, and the Bull & Last in Highgate can definitely stake a claim to being the spiritual home of the gastropub Scotch egg thanks to the dedication of chef and owner Ollie Pudney in creating a bar snack that is alone worth the trip to Highgate. The Bull & Last is an imposing corner pub, with diners welcome in both the main bar and upstairs restaurant. The menu has a strong focus on the very best British meat and game, along with fresh and seasonal produce sourced from artisan suppliers. The chefs can even be seen out on Hampstead Heath from time-to-time, foraging for the day's menu. Breakfast is served at weekends.

Après une longue traversée de désert (gastronomique), les « plats de comptoir » retrouvent leur lustre à Londres, certains chefs ayant la bonne idée de réhabiliter et revisiter tourtes ou autres grattons de porc. Cette adresse, dirigée par le chef et propriétaire Ollie Pudney, peut ainsi se targuer d'être le berceau du renouveau du Scotch egg (un œuf dur entouré de farce), traité ici façon « gastropub ». Dans cette adresse imposante qui accueille les clients sur deux étages, la carte propose également ce qui se fait de mieux en matière de viande et gibier britanniques, mais aussi de fruits et légumes tous issus de petits producteurs. Et, certains jours, vous rencontrerez à Hampstead Heath la brigade en train de cueillir les ingrédients destinés au menu du jour ! À noter qu'un petit-déjeuner est servi le week-end.

À la carte : Crispy pig cheek, watermelon pickle, basil and sesame / *Joue de porc croustillante, condiment à la pastèque, basilic et sésame* 9 £ • Grilled tiger prawns, monksbeard, chilli, lemon and aioli / *Gambas tigre grillées, pousses vertes, piment, citron et aïoli* 9,75 £ 21 £ • Beer battered haddock, chips, pea puree and tartare sauce / *Haddock pané à la bière, frites, purée de petit-pois et sauce tartare* 15 £ • Bramley apple crumble, vanilla ice cream and clotted cream / *Crumble de pommes Bramley, glace vanille et crème épaisse* 7,50 £.
Closed Mondays / *Fermé le lundi*

THE CANONBURY

21 Canonbury Place, London N1 2NS
Tube / *Métro* : Highbury & Islington (Victoria)
+44 20 7704 2887
www.thecanonbury.co.uk

There has been a pub on the site of the Canonbury since the early 1700s and the current building dates back to the 1840s. The Canonbury has one of the best pub gardens in London, and author George Orwell, who lived nearby, wrote part of 1984 while sitting under one of its trees. London pub company

Young's acquired the Canonbury recently, and reopened it after refurbishment inside and out in May 2015. Oisin Rogers, who previously ran the hugely successful Ship in Wandsworth, is now in charge. The pub has a main dining area as well as a private dining room, with a menu that focuses on seasonal British ingredients, with a grill menu as well as the main food offer. The drinks range includes a wide choice of real ales and craft beers, along with an interesting choice of wine.

À cette adresse existe un pub depuis le début du 18ème siècle et le bâtiment actuel date d'environ 1840. Le Canonbury possède un des plus agréables jardins de Londres, et George Orwell qui habitait dans le quartier, y a d'ailleurs écrit une partie de 1984 assis sous un arbre... La dernière actualité, c'est sa reprise par Young's qui l'a complètement remis à neuf avant de le rouvrir en mai 2015 et d'en confier les rênes à Oisin Rogers qui tenait précédemment le réputé Ship à Wandsworth. Ce pub dont une salle peut être privatisée, propose une cuisine qui sait mettre en valeur des produits de saison bien britanniques avec une carte dédiée aux seules grillades. Pour les boissons, vous avez le choix entre une large sélection de bières aussi authentiques qu'artisanales, et un choix de vins tout aussi pertinent.

À la carte : Clams steamed in garlic and lemon butter with parsley cornbread / *Palourdes vapeur au beurre d'ail et citron, avec pain au maïs et au persil* 8 £ • Pulled pork shoulder sandwich with coleslaw and fries (grill) / *Sandwich au porc confit, coleslaw et frites* 12 £ • Rib eye steak with red wine jus, crouton and thick-cut chips (300g) / *Faux filet, sauce au vin rouge, croûton et grosses frites* 26 £ • Seared sea bass with warm cucumber salad, grapes and pine kernel crust / *Bar grillé, salade tiède de concombre, croûte aux raisins et aux pignons* 15 £ • Elderflower panna cotta with strawberries, mint and muscat / *Panna cotta à la fleur de sureau, fraises, menthe et muscat* 7 £.
Open every day / *Ouvert tous les jours*

🍴 THE DRAPERS ARMS

🏠 44 Barnsbury St, Islington, London N1 1ER
Tube / *Métro* : Highbury & Islington (Victoria)
+ 44 20 7619 0348
www.thedrapersarms.com

The Draper's Arms has been a feature of Islington's social scene since 1839 and, as the name suggests, the freehold is owned by the Worshipful Company of Drapers, one of London's historic livery companies. The pub was acquired by restaurateur Nick Gibson in 2009 and reopened as a modern gastropub with a focus on seasonal produce. The elegant building includes a bar, restaurant and private dining area, as well as a secluded terrace garden. The bar menu includes traditional London seafood specialities such as rock oysters and whelks, while the main menu features good value dishes made with high quality meat and game, as well as fresh fish. The wine list includes a selection of excellent regional wines, and there is a small but high quality choice of British cask ales.

Cette institution d'Islington depuis 1839 est, comme son nom l'indique, liée à la vieille compagnie de drapiers de Londres. Ce pub a été repris en 2009 par le restaurateur Nick Gibson pour devenir un « gastropub » contemporain qui fait la part belle aux produits de saison. Le bâtiment au demeurant élégant comprend un bar, un restaurant avec partie privatisable, ainsi qu'un jardin-terrasse bien à l'abri des regards. S'il est possible au bar de déguster des huîtres ou coquillages comme on les aime à Londres, la carte principale propose tout autant viande ou gibier de qualité que poisson de grande fraîcheur, le tout à des prix restés corrects. Carte des vins bien pourvue en crus régionaux et sélection pointue de bières britanniques.

À la carte : Deep fried quail, aioli and pickled chillies / *Cailles frites, aïoli, piments au vinaigre* 7,50 £ • Pork and duck rillettes, toast and pickles / *Rillettes de porc et canard, pain grillé et cornichons* 6,50 £ • Monkfish, bacon, broad beans and rosemary / *Lotte, bacon, fèves et romarin* 16,50 £ • Whole mackerel, grilled fennel and gooseberry sauce / *Maquereau entier, fenouil grillé, sauce à la groseille à maquereau* 15,50 £ • Chocolate and caramel pot, shortbread crumble and strawberries / *Petit pot au chocolat et caramel, crumble de sablés et fraises* 6,50 £.
Open every day / *Ouvert tous les jours*

🍲 THE FLASK
🍲 77 Highgate West Hill, Camden, London N6 6BU
Tube / *Métro* : Highgate (Northern)
+ 44 20 8348 7346
www.theflaskhighgate.com

Highgate and Hampstead have no shortage of historic pubs, but the Flask has a good claim to be one of the finest. Named for the flasks sold by enterprising salesmen to allow Londoners who made it up the hill to collect clean spring water in the days when the water supply down in the city was poisonous, the main part of the pub was built in the 1720s. Poet Samuel Coleridge and artist William Hogarth are some of the former regulars, and the Flask even claims to have a few ghosts, including a barmaid and a cavalier. Owner Fullers has kept the pub as it always was, with many small bar areas and dining rooms, and the food also reflects the heritage with a range of freshly cooked, seasonal British dishes that have a definite timeless feel, while still modern enough to appeal to both local and visitors.

Si les quartiers de Highgate et Hampstead ne manquent pas de pubs historiques, nul doute, le Flask est le meilleur ! Construit pour sa partie principale en 1720, il tire son nom des bouteilles ou flasques que proposaient des vendeurs avisés aux Londoniens prêts à grimper la côte pour s'approvisionner en eau de source... Et pour continuer sur une note historique, le poète Samuel Coleridge comme l'artiste William Hogarth avaient ici leurs habitudes. Et sachez aussi que l'adresse hébergerait toujours quelques fantômes, une serveuse et un cavalier notamment ! Fullers, le propriétaire, a heureusement conservé au pub son authenticité (ses contes et légendes aussi !), comme ses nombreux coins et recoins qu'occupent bar ou salle à manger. La cuisine reste fidèle à cet héritage du passé avec des recettes bien anglaises, presque hors du temps, sans oublier parfois une touche plus contemporaine pour fidéliser ou attirer le client

À la carte : Clam and smoked haddock chowder, onion sourdough / *Soupe de palourdes et haddock fumé, pain au levain à l'oignon* 6,50 £ • Earl Grey smoked wood pigeon breast, remoulade and drunken prunes / *Poitrine de pigeon sauvage fumée à l'Earl Grey, rémoulade et pruneaux ivres* 8,50 £ • Spiced lamb burger, tzatziki, harissa mayonnaise and chips / *Burger d'agneau*

épicé, tzatziki, mayonnaise à l'harissa, frites 12,75 £ • Pan roasted
Loch Duarte salmon, crushed Jersey Royals, langoustine bisque /
*Saumon du Loch Duarte poêlé, écrasée de pommes de terre Jersey
Royal, bisque de langoustines* 14,95 £ • Sticky toffee pudding
and vanilla ice cream / *Sticky toffee pudding et glace vanille* 6 £.
Open every day / *Ouvert tous les jours*

🐌 HEIRLOOM
🐌 35 Park Road, Crouch End, London N8 8TE
🐌 Tube / *Métro* : Highgate (Northern)
 +44 20 8348 3565
 www.heirloomn8.co.uk

Crouch End is about as far north in London as this guide
goes, but it is definitely worth an extra stop or two on
the tube to experience this collaboration between award
winning chef Chris Slaughter, and produce-growers David
and Ian Macintosh. The heart of the menu is the range
of interesting and often unusual vegetables grown by the
McIntosh brothers on Hazeldene Farm, Buckinghamshire.
Produce is picked daily and the website updated to show
the produce available. The vegetables accompany rare breed
meat cuts and freshly caught fish, and the menu changes
daily to reflect the different combinations in which pro-
duce can be lovingly cooked, and the Sunday roast lunches
are especially worth a visit. The wine list includes bio-
dynamic wines, with a craft beer range on offer alongside a
bar menu geared towards sharing plates.

*Situé à Crouch End, à l'extrême nord de la zone couverte
par le guide, osez prolonger le voyage d'une ou deux sta-
tions de métro pour profiter de cette adresse née de la
rencontre entre Chris Slaughter, chef primé, et David et
Ian Macintosh, maraîchers. La cuisine met donc en va-
leur la sélection de légumes pointus et souvent méconnus
que les frères Macintosh font pousser dans leur ferme
de Hazeldene dans le Buckinghamshire. Leur production
quotidienne - un site internet permet de suivre les der-
nières récoltes - accompagne à merveille pièces de viande
issues de races souvent rares ou poissons d'une évidente
fraîcheur. La carte change tous les jours et propose avec
amour des préparations à chaque fois différentes. Sans
oublier les rôtis servis au déjeuner du dimanche qui*

*méritent à eux seuls le voyage. ! Enfin, au bar, possibilité
de déguster des assiettes à partager. Sélection de vins en
biodynamie et bières artisanales.*

À la carte : Game terrine, kohlrabi salad and crispy duck fritter /
Terrine de gibier, salade de chou frisé, croustillant de canard
8,50 £ • Tandoori sea trout rillettes, provence tomatoes, African
basil and crostini / *Rillettes de truite tandoori, tomates de Provence,
basilic africain et crostini* 9 £ • Grass-fed lamb saddle, Tokyo tur-
nips, jersey royal salad, roasted shallot and vadovan sauce / *Selle
d'agneau broutard, navets de Tokyo, salade de pommes de terre
Jersey Royal, échalote rôtie, sauce au Vadouvan* 19,50 £ • Cornish
cod, Russian kale, skordalia, farm beetroots and romesco sauce /
*Cabillaud de Cornouaille, chou kale de Russie, skordalia, betteraves
fermières, sauce romesco* 19 £ • Nicoise lemon posset, gooseberry
and apple marigold compote and shortbread / *« Posset » au citron
niçois, compote aux groseilles à maquereau et à l'herbe « apple
marigold », sablé* 6,50 £.
Closed Mondays and Tuesdays / *Fermé le lundi et le mardi*

☕ THE HOLLY BUSH

22 Hollymount, Hampstead, London NW3 6SG
Tube / *Métro* : Hampstead (Northern)
+44 20 7435 2892
www.hollybushhampstead.co.uk

**Hampstead has no shortage of historic pubs, thanks to
its status as one of the traditional getaway locations for
London's more affluent residents, high on a hill overloo-
king the City to the south. The Holly Bush in Hampstead
village is more than 200 years old, a Georgian building with
an authentic feel inside thanks to original features such
as dark wooden floors and tables. London brewer Fuller's
acquired the pub in 2010 and has updated the menu to
feature freshly cooked dishes and high quality seasonal in-
gredients alongside classic pub food. As well as the main
restaurant, the Holly Bush has a choice of private dining,
from a small room to large function areas. In winter, the
pub is a wonderful place to sit in front of an open fire with
a pint of cask ale and a bar meal, and enjoy the many items
of local history that decorate the walls.**

Du haut de sa colline qui surplombe le sud de la ville, Hampstead a toujours été un lieu de promenade apprécié des riches Londoniens. De nombreux pubs s'y sont installés, comme ce Holly Bush, vieux de plus de 200 ans. Avec son architecture géorgienne, son parquet et ses tables en bois d'origine, il a conservé une atmosphère authentique. Et, quant en 2010 le brasseur londonien Fuller's en devient propriétaire, ce dernier a la bonne idée d'ajouter aux plats traditionnels une carte riche en spécialités maison et ingrédients de saison. En hiver, on profitera du feu de cheminée comme des nombreux souvenirs qui ornent les murs, tout en dégustant un plat accompagné d'une bonne pinte de bière. À noter que certains espaces sont privatisables.

À la carte : Grilled herring fillet, black focaccia, salsa verde, tomato sorbet, parmesan / *Filet de hareng grillé, foccacia noire, salsa verde, sorbet tomate, parmesan* 9,50 £ • Rib eye steak, café de Paris butter, herb salad, hand cut chips and green peppercorn sauce / *Faux filet, beurre Café de Paris, salade d'herbes, frites coupées à la main, sauce au poivre* 25 £ • Yorkshire rhubarb and apple crumble ginger ice cream / *Crumble de rhubarbe du Yorkshire et de pomme, glace au gingembre* 6,50 £.
Open every day / *Ouvert tous les jours*

☕ THE PARCEL YARD
☕ King's Cross Station, London, N1C 4AH
Tube / *Métro* : Kings Cross (Victoria/Circle/District/Piccadilly/Metropolitan)
+ 44 20 7713 7258
www.parcelyard.co.uk

Located in Kings Cross Station, the entrance to the Parcel Yard is up a flight of stairs close to Platform 9¾, from where Harry Potter caught the Hogwarts Express. The pub was redeveloped by London brewer Fuller's during the recent major upgrade to King's Cross, and has seen the station's old parcel distribution depot converted into a two-storey pub and dining rooms with a number of different areas, including private dining and meeting rooms, while retaining many original features of the building. Popular with travellers and for business meetings, the menu at the Parcel Yard features fresh, seasonal British food with plenty of interesting small plate choices, while the substantial English

breakfast is worth braving London's rush hour for. The bar offers a wide selection of cask ale and craft beers, as well as wines from Fuller's own range.

Dans la gare de Kings Cross, l'entrée du Parcel Yard se fait en haut de l'escalier qui jouxte le fameux quai 9¾ d'où Harry Potter prit le train pour Hogwarts. Repris en main par le brasseur Fuller's lors de la rénovation de la gare, l'ancien centre de distribution des colis est ainsi devenu un pub qui, sur deux étages, distille ses salles à manger, certaines privatisables ou transformables en salles de réunion, toutes ayant conservé de nombreux éléments du bâtiment d'origine. La carte a de quoi ravir voyageurs et hommes d'affaires, avec un registre bien britannique qui fait la part belle aux saisons et des assiettes toujours bien troussées. Ne pas faire l'impasse sur le copieux breakfast anglais qui, aux heures matinales de pointe, mérite de savoir patienter... Au bar, large sélection de bières de fût artisanales ainsi que de vins issues de la sélection Fuller's.

À la carte : London porter smoked salmon, celeriac and horseradish remoulade, potato bread / *Saumon fumé London Porter, rémoulade de céleri et raifort, pain à la pomme de terre* 7,50 £ • Chicken, ham and apricot terrine, balsamic onions and toasted bread / *Terrine de poulet, jambon et abricots, oignons au balsamique, pain grillé* 6,95 £ • Pear, apple and cinnamon crumble, vanilla custard / *Crumble de pomme, poire et cannelle, crème anglaise à la vanille* 5,95 £.
Open every day / *Ouvert tous les jours*

🍽 THE PARLOUR
🍽 5 Regent Street, London, NW10 5LG
Tube / *Métro* : Kensall Green (Bakerloo)
+ 44 20 8969 2184
www.parlourkensal.com

The Parlour is a modern neighbourhood restaurant, located out to the west in Kensal Green. The menu, overseen by chef Jesse Dunford Wood, changes weekly and includes a mix of seasonal dishes and British classics. The all-day dining offer starts with brunch and goes right through to midnight, with set price options for both lunch and dinner.

The menu has a focus on contemporary comfort food, including Jesse Dunford Wood's signature cow pie, named for the dish eaten by British comic strip character Desperate Dan, and made with delicious chucks of beef in a rich gravy under a crumbly pie crust. The Chef's Table seats seven people, while for 10 or more there is the option to share starters and puddings. The drinks menu is designed to complement the food and includes light lunchtime cocktails as well as a well-selected range of unusual craft beers.

Voilà un restaurant de quartier, moderne, situé vers l'ouest à Kensal Green et dont la carte, supervisée par le chef Jesse Dunford Wood, change toutes les semaines et s'inspire autant des saisons que des classiques du répertoire culinaire britannique. On peut y prendre un repas toute la journée, du brunch jusqu'à minuit, avec des formules bien étudiées au déjeuner comme au dîner. Le registre défend une cuisine à la fois contemporaine et réconfortante. La « cow pie » (tourte de vache) en est le plat signature - l'intitulé est en fait emprunté à la recette dégustée par Desperate Dan, personnage de bande dessinée britannique - avec une pâte légère garnie de délicieux morceaux de bœuf et d'une riche sauce. Si la table du chef accueille sept personnes, il est possible à dix, voire plus, d'y partager entrées ou desserts. Quant aux boissons de la carte, elles sont choisies pour accompagner les plats, avec notamment des cocktails légers pour le déjeuner et des bières artisanales étonnantes.

À la carte : Grilled English asparagus and fried bread crumbs / *Asperges anglaises grillées, chapelure frite* 8,50 £ • Duck liver pate, cold toast and marmalade / *Pâté de foie de canard, toast froid et marmelade* 7 £ • "Remarkable" pork chop, tomato and basil salad / *« Remarquable » côte de porc, salade de tomates et basilic* 17 £ • Sea trout, samphire, asparagus and seaweed / *Truite de mer, salicorne, asperges et algues* 16 £ • Hot strawberry souffle with pink praline / *Soufflé chaud aux fraises avec des pralines roses* 8 £.
Closed Mondays / *Fermé le lundi*

🐷 THE PIG AND BUTCHER

🐷 80 Liverpool Rd, Islington, London N1 0QD
🎩 Tube / *Métro :* Angel (Northern)
   + 44 20 7226 8304
   www.thepigandbutcher.co.uk

Located in an imposing Victorian pub, the Pig and Butcher celebrates Islington's former status as the farmland where livestock being moved into London were grazed on the way to their final destination at Smithfield Meat Market. The pub takes delivery of whole carcasses and prepares them on site. The focus is rare breeds including White Park cattle, Iron Age pigs and Hebridean lamb, along with game from Chart Farm in Kent. Both the menu and cooking styles change with the seasons, with food grilled over charcoal and wood in summer, while in winter meat is cured, smoked and braised to create delicious, comforting dishes. Fish dishes are decided according to the day's catch. The food is prepared fresh and simply, reflecting both British and European influences, with small plate options for those who want to share. The Pig and Butcher is part of the Noble Inn gastropub group.

> *Cet imposant pub victorien célèbre à sa façon l'époque où sur les pâturages d'Islington broutait le bétail qui rejoignait ensuite Londres et le marché de viande de Smithfield, sa destination finale. Aujourd'hui, le Pig and Butcher se fait livrer des carcasses entières, les prépare sur place et privilégie les origines de qualité : race White Park, cochons Iron Age, agneau des îles Hébrides ou gibier de Chart Farm dans le Kent. La cuisine et les méthodes de cuisson varient selon les saisons, grillades au charbon ou au bois en été, viande séchée, fumée ou braisée pour des plats aussi délicieux que réconfortants en hiver. Quant aux poissons servis, ils restent de la même façon tributaires de la pêche du jour. Tout est donc frais, simple, dans un registre à la fois britannique et continentale, avec aussi de petites portions pour ceux qui veulent partager.*

À la carte : Rabbit rillettes, cornichons and toast / *Rillettes de lapin, cornichons et pain grillé* 7,25 £ • Cornish octopus, pineapple tomato and fregola / *Poulpe de Cornouaille, tomate ananas et fregola* 7,25 £ • Angus onglet, chimichurri and double dipped chips / *Onglet de bœuf Angus, chimichurri et frites cuites deux fois* 17,50 £ • Grilled Brixham plaice, new potatoes and

green sauce / *Plie de Brixham grillée, pommes de terre nouvelles et sauce verte* 15,50 £ • Caramelised chocolate mousse, cashew crumble and vanilla ice cream / *Mousse au chocolat caramélisée, crumble de noix de cajou et glace vanille* 6,50 £ • Grilled white peach, lemon verbena, bee pollen and clotted cream ice cream / *Pêche blanche grillée, verveine citronnée, pollen d'abeille et glace à la crème épaisse* 6,50 £.
Open every day / *Ouvert tous les jours*

⬤ SEASON KITCHEN & DINING ROOM
⬤ 53 Stroud Green Rd, London N4 3EF
⬤ Tube / *Métro :* Manor House (Piccadilly)
 +44 20 7263 5500
 www.seasonkitchen.co.uk

The unassuming high street location in Finsbury Park doesn't do Season Kitchen & Dining Room any favours, but the eclectic and interesting menu at this independently owned business is well worth seeking out. As the name suggests, both the ingredients and menu aim to follow the seasons with the highest quality fresh food. Alongside British dishes, the menu takes inspiration from France and Italy as well as further afield. Food is sourced as locally as possible with an emphasis on keeping food miles to a minimum. The 'Cheapsteak Tuesday' promotion featuring unusual cuts of beef is always interesting, the home baked bread is excellent, and the wine list is great value.

C'est dans une rue commerçante et sans prétention de Finsbury Park qu'il faut aller dénicher ce Season Kitchen & Dining Room à la carte pourtant éclectique et prometteuse. Comme son nom le suggère, la cuisine fait honneur aux meilleurs produits comme aux saisons. Elle ne se limite d'ailleurs pas aux seuls plats britanniques, la carte puisant son inspiration aussi en France, en Italie, voire même plus loin. Tout est confectionné dès que possible à base de produits des environs avec, à la clé, un rapport « kilomètres nourriture », au plus bas. Le mardi, c'est jour du « Cheapsteak » une invitation à déguster dans les meilleures conditions des pièces de bœuf souvent méconnues. Excellent pain maison et sélection de vins d'un bon rapport qualité – prix.

À la carte : Duck ham with figs and mascarpone / *Jambon de canard avec figues et mascarpone* 6,50 £ • Mackerel with chargrilled hispi cabbage and almond mayo / *Maquereau au chou pointu Hispi et mayonnaise à l'amande* 6,50 £ • Pulled kid with ramsons, sweet cicely and cobnuts / *Agneau confit, ail des ours, herbes « sweet cicely », noisettes* 15,95 £ • Wild brown trout with clams, sea vegetables and broth / *Truite fario sauvage avec palourdes, légumes de la mer et bouillon* 15,50 £ • Rosemary chocolate pot with black pepper biscotti / *Petit pot au chocolat et au romarin avec biscotti au poivre noir* 5,95 £ • Buttermilk pannacotta with crumble and blood orange jelly / *Pannacotta au lait ribot avec crumble et gelée d'oranges sanguines* 5,95 £.
Closed Mondays / *Fermé le lundi*

☺ SMOKEHOUSE
☺ 63–69 Canonbury Rd, Islington, London, N1 2DG
☺ Tube / *Métro :* Highbury & Islington (Victoria)
+44 20 7354 1144
www.smokehouseislington.co.uk

As London food critic Fay Maschler put it, "this is the place to show us why man discovered fire". Many London restaurants have followed the trend for smoked and barbecued dishes, but Smokehouse in Islington is the place of pilgrimage for London's smoked food fraternity. Part of the Noble Inns gastropub group, the drinks side of the business is worth a trip in its own right, with a wide range of draught and bottled beers – including smoked beers, naturally – along with a well-chosen wine list. Under the watchful eye of head chef Neil Rankin, delicious cuts of meat and meat and fish are smoked on site, and food is served from a busy open kitchen. A second Smokehouse has opened to the west in Chiswick.

Comme l'a écrit Fay Maschler, critique gastronomique londonienne, « voilà la parfaite adresse pour comprendre pourquoi l'homme a eu besoin du feu ». Si d'autres adresses ont suivi cet engouement pour les plats fumés et autres barbecues, le Smokehouse reste le lieu de pèlerinage des Londoniens qui apprécient un tel registre. Sous l'œil attentif du chef Neil Rankin, viandes et poissons, tous délicieux, sont fumés sur place avant d'être préparés depuis la cuisine ouverte et toujours animée. Propriété du Noble Inns gastropub group, les boissons ne sont surtout pas oubliées, avec une belle sélection de bières pression ou en bouteille – comprenant bien entendu des bières fumées ! – et une carte des vins bien choisie. Bon à savoir, un second Smokehouse a ouvert vers l'ouest à Chiswick.

À la carte : Deep fried rock oyster, beef dripping toast, smoked bone marrow / *Huîtres frites, toast au jus de bœuf, moelle fumée* 8 £ • Grilled salmon and Thai salad / *Salade thaï au saumon grillé* 16 £ • Shortrib bourguignon / *Bourguignon de plat de côtes* 18 £ • Rum and raisin rice pudding, blackberry jam and almonds / *Riz au lait rhum raisin, confiture de mûres et amandes* 6,50 £.
Open every day / *Ouvert tous les jours*

West London

🍽 THE ABINGDON
🍲 54 Abingdon Road, London, W8 6AP
Tube / *Métro :* High Street Kensington (Circle/District)
+44 20 7937 3339
www.theabingdon.co.uk

....

Located in a residential street in West London, the Abingdon describes itself as "Kensington's little secret". The building still looks like a traditional London street corner pub, but inside it has reinvented itself as a stylish modern family restaurant and wine bar. There is a large bar area with cushions and sofas as well as tables, a conventional restaurant area, and a rear dining area with red leather booths. The family-owned pub specialises in modern European food, often with a more exotic and spicy twist, with many dishes cooked in a charcoal oven, including the occasional superb tandoori. Both lunch and evening menus change daily. The wine list specialises in the new world, and instead of draught beer there is an unusual selection of bottled beers, including excellent German imports.

Situé dans une rue résidentielle de l'ouest de Londres, l'Abingdon se présente comme « l'adresse secrète de Kensington ». Si le bâtiment revêt les habits d'un pub traditionnel de Londres, l'intérieur ressemble plus à celui d'un restaurant familial et bar à vins au goût bien contemporain. Autour du comptoir, canapés, coussins mais aussi tables occupent un vaste espace, avec, un peu plus loin, une salle de restaurant classique et, à l'arrière, une autre aux alcôves tout habillées de cuir rouge. Ce pub qui est la propriété d'une famille, s'est spécialisé dans une cuisine européenne contemporaine aux touches parfois exotiques et épicées, avec de nombreux plats cuits au four à charbon, et, parfois, de superbes tandoori. Les cartes du midi comme du soir changent tous les jours. La sélection de vins met le cap sur le nouveau monde et celle de bières, de façon inhabituelle, privilégie aux pressions les bouteilles, avec notamment d'excellentes importées d'Allemagne.

À la carte : Warm beef salad with new potatoes and cornichon dressing / *Salade de bœuf tiède avec pommes de terre nouvelles et vinaigrette aux cornichons* 8 £ • Tempura of wild halibut with and

soft shell crab with lemongrass dip and soy / *Tempura de flétan et crabe mou, sauce à la citronnelle et au soja* 10,40 £ • Roasted black pig pork belly with mustard mash, fine beans, caramelized shallots / *Poitrine de porc rôtie, purée à la moutarde, haricots verts extra fins, échalotes caramélisées* 17,50 £ • North sea cod with truffle mash, courgette, sea spinach, baby fennel and confit tomato / *Cabillaud de la mer du Nord, purée à la truffe, courgettes, épinards de mer, fenouil nouveau et tomate confite* 21,50 £ • Sticky toffee pudding with toffee sauce and clotted cream / *Sticky toffee pudding avec sauce au café et crème épaisse.*
Open every day / *Ouvert tous les jours*

🥟 BARNYARD
🥟 18 Charlotte Street London W1T 2LZ
🥟 Tube / *Métro :* Goodge Street (Northern)
+ 44 20 7580 3842
http://barnyard-london.com

Fitzrovia has long been the location for many of London's more interesting bistro and wine bars, and Barnyard continues the tradition. The name is reflected in the rustic wooden décor as well as the tin plates on which the food is served. However, the dedication of chef Ollie Dabbous to creating new and imaginative twists on traditional British dishes more than makes up for the occasional feel of a theme restaurant. There's no booking at Barnyard, so diners should expect to queue for a table at busy times, but this is an opportunity to wait at the bar and explore a drinks menu which includes craft beer, mead and cider, home-made fruit shandies, and delicious alcoholic milkshakes served in milk bottles, such as Gingerbread with Golden Rum.

Fitzrovia est depuis longtemps réputé pour ses bistrots et bars à vins, et le Barnyard perpétue bien la tradition. Son nom (basse-cour) explique certainement le décor rustique en bois comme les assiettes en fer blanc dans lesquelles sont servis les plats. Mais loin d'être un restaurant à thème, le chef Ollie Dabbous revisite avec à propos et originalité les plats traditionnels britanniques. Le Barnyard ne prenant pas de réservations, vous risquez de faire la queue pour avoir une table aux heures de pointe. Profitez-en pour patienter au bar et parcourir la carte

des boissons : elle propose, entre autres, bières artisa-
nales, hydromel, cidre, panachés aux fruits maison et milk
shakes alcoolisés servis dans des bouteilles de lait, tous
délicieux comme celui au pain d'épices et au rhum ambré !

À la carte : Homemade sausage roll with piccalilli / *Sandwich à*
la saucisse maison, condiment Piccalilli 8 £ • Barbecued bavette,
homemade dill pickle, mustard and black treacle / *Bavette au*
barbecue, cornichons maison à l'aneth, moutarde et mélasse noire
15 £ • Roast suckling pig with celeriac and caraway / *Cochon de*
lait rôti avec du céleri et du carvi 13 £ • Lemon posset with mar-
joram / *« Posset » au citron et à la marjolaine* 6 £.
Open every day / *Ouvert tous les jours*

🐄 THE COW (WESTBOURNE PARK RD)

🐄 89 Westbourne Park Rd, London, W2 5QH
🐄 Tube / *Métro :* Westbourne Park (Bakerloo/Waterloo)
+ 44 20 7221 0021
www.thecowlondon.co.uk

The inspiration for many other London gastropubs, the Cow was
set up by restaurateur Tom Conran in 1995, and is one of the
eating out venues that helped to make the Notting Hill Gate
area popular with the younger affluent London crowd. It still
has the feel of a venue where bright young things meet to enjoy
drinks, a meal and good times with friends. The ground floor
pub and first floor restaurant have different styles, but the
overall feel is casual and lively. The menu style is a mix of pub
classics and modern British dishes. Farm-sourced meat and
game, especially the beef, are excellent, and the hearty pies are
worth the trip on cold days. The Cow also makes a speciality of
seafood, including oysters and a fish of the day. The wine list
is priced towards the top end for a pub, but definitely worth
exploring.

Créé par le restaurateur Tom Conran en 1995, le Cow
a ouvert la voie à de nombreux gastropubs de Londres
comme il a permis à Notting Hill de devenir l'un des quar-
tiers appréciés des jeunes Londoniens aisés. L'ambiance
est toujours là et la jeunesse dorée s'y retrouve volon-
tiers pour boire un verre ou prendre un repas entre amis.
Si le pub au rez-de-chaussée et le restaurant à l'étage
offrent des univers différents, ils partagent une même

atmosphère, détendue et enjouée. La carte réunit les classiques du pub anglais et en même temps propose des plats au registre beaucoup plus contemporain. On se régale ici de gibier, de viande, notamment de bœuf en provenance de petits éleveurs, mais aussi de généreuses tourtes quand il fait froid. Le Cow est également réputé pour ses fruits de mer, huîtres ou poissons du jour. La carte des vins se situe dans le haut de la fourchette des prix pour un pub, mais mérite de s'y attarder.

À la carte : Paté de la maison, piccalilli, toast / *Pâté maison, condiment Piccalilli, pain grillé* 9 £ • Home smoked salmon, beetroot, potato and dill salad, horseradish crème fraîche / *Saumon fumé maison, betteraves, salade de pommes de terre à l'aneth, crème fraîche au raifort* 9,50 £ • Beef and guinness pie, suet crust, buttered greens / *Tourte au bœuf et à la Guinness, croûte au saindoux, embeurrée de légumes verts* 13 £ • Cow fish stew, rouille and crouton / *Ragoût de poisson du Cow, rouille et croûtons* 16 £ • Blackberry and apple crumble, custard / *Crumble de mûre et pomme, crème anglaise* 6,50 £.
Open every day / *Ouvert tous les jours*

🥟 DUCK & RICE
🥟 90 Berwick Street, Soho W1F 0QB
Tube / *Métro :* Piccadilly Circus (Piccadilly/Bakerloo)
+44 20 3327 7888
www.theduckandrice.com

Bringing a genuinely new concept to the Soho eating out scene, restaurateur Alan Yau has transformed a run-down Soho pub into the Duck & Rice, London's first Chinese gastropub. The ground floor has a classic pub feel, with a focus on craft beer including cask Pilsner Urquell, and has a real buzz at lunchtime and early evening with people who live and work in Soho meeting for drinks. Selections from the 'Small Chow' menu make ideal bar food, including a bowl of spicy Chilli Sichuan Chicken that is definitely not for the faint-hearted and needs a cold beer to accompany it. The upstairs restaurant has a more elegant feel, and serves a wide variety of expertly prepared and cooked Chinese dishes using fresh, high quality ingredients. The Duck & Rice House Special is Lobster Cantonese, and the tempting Ten Heavenly Kings of Dim Sum selection leads to some difficult choices.

Le restaurateur Alan Yau a offert un concept vraiment novateur à la scène gastronomique de Soho en reprenant un pub délabré pour en faire le premier gastropub chinois de Londres. Au rez-de-chaussée, une ambiance classique avec un bon choix de bières artisanales, y compris de la Pilsner Urquell en fût, vite animée quand à midi et en début de soirée s'y retrouvent pour y boire un verre ceux qui habitent ou travaillent à Soho. Les petites portions de la carte « Small Chow » sont alors parfaites pour grignoter au bar, notamment le poulet pimenté à la sichuanaise, à déconseiller cependant aux palais délicats et à déguster sans faute avec une bière bien fraîche... À l'étage, le restaurant se montre plus élégant et propose un grand choix de plats chinois, tous parfaitement exécutés à partir d'ingrédients d'une indéniable fraîcheur et qualité. La spécialité du Duck & Rice reste le homard cantonnais, et la sélection tout aussi appétissante des « dix rois du paradis des dim sum » ne facilite certes pas le choix...

À la carte : Pan-fried pork and Chinese leaves gyoza / *Gyozas au porc et au chou chinois poêlés* 5,50 £ • Crabmeat and sweetcorn soup / *Soupe au crabe et au maïs doux* 9 £ • Chicken chop suey / *Chop suey au poulet* 12,50 £ • Jasmine smoked pork rib / *Travers de porc fumé au jasmin* 14 £ • Papaya with vanilla ice cream / *Papaye à la glace vanille* 6 £.
Open every day / *Ouvert tous les jours*

🎩 GRAZING GOAT

🎩 6 New Quebec St. W1H 7RQ
Tube / *Métro* : Marble Arch (Central)
+44 20 7724 7243
www.thegrazinggoat.co.uk

Located in the Portman Village area close to Marble Arch, the Grazing Goat aims to bring the feel of a country house weekend to central London. The regency building includes eight boutique hotel rooms, which adds to the getaway feel. The downstairs bar comes closest to the original pub feel, with an upmarket bar menu, while the upstairs restaurant has a more formal feel. The menu crosses the boundaries of the two, with bar meals often doing double duty as starters upstairs. The focus is very much on lovingly prepared meat dishes, with game and rare breed pork and beef often featuring on the special rotisserie and grill menu. A fish of the day choice is also available. The business is run by the Cubitt Group, which also operates the Thomas Cubitt in Belgravia and other upmarket London eateries.

Dans le quartier de Portman Village, près de Marble Arch, le Grazing Goat tente de recréer en plein cœur de Londres l'ambiance d'un week-end dans une maison de campagne. Le bâtiment régence héberge également huit chambres d'un hôtel-boutique qui participent à leur façon à cette impression d'évasion. Au rez-de-chaussée, le bar reproduit à la perfection l'ambiance d'un pub avec une carte d'encas plutôt haut de gamme quand, au dessus, le restaurant distille une ambiance plus solennelle. La carte fait le lien entre les deux étages, les assiettes du bar étant également proposées en entrée au restaurant. La cuisine fait honneur à la viande, gibier, porc ou bœuf de race, tous préparés avec amour et souvent proposés sur la carte des grillades ou rôtisseries. À noter qu'un poisson du marché est chaque jour proposé au menu. Bon à savoir, l'affaire est gérée par le groupe Cubitt, qui à la charge du Thomas Cubitt à Belgravia comme d'autres établissements haut de gamme de Londres.

À la carte : Potted pork, apricot chutney, cider brandy and toast (bar menu) / *Verrine de porc, chutney à l'abricot, alcool de pomme et pain grillé* 9 £ • Rare breed beef burger, red onion, three cheese chorizo sauce / *Burger de bœuf de race rare, oignon rouge, sauce chorizo et trois fromages* 14,50 £ • Suffolk chicken, bacon and sage stuffing / *Poulet du Suffolk farci au bacon et à la sauge* 14,50 £ • Pan fried hake, black pepper and truffle dumplings, shallots, brown shrimp dressing / *Merlu poêlé, quenelles au poivre noir et à la truffe, échalotes, vinaigrette à la crevette* 17 £ • Thyme roasted peach, soft meringue, iced almond parfait / *Pêche rôtie au thym, meringue moelleuse, parfait glacé à l'amande* 7 £.
Open every day / *Ouvert tous les jours*

🍲 THE GUINEA

30 Bruton Place W1J 6NL
Tube / *Métro* : Green Park (Victoria/Jubilee)
+ 44 20 7499 1210
www.theguinea.co.uk

The guinea, or one pound and one shilling, was the traditional English gentleman's preferred unit of currency. The Guinea Grill opened in Mayfair, close to Berkeley Square in 1952, although there has been an inn on the site since 1423. This is the place to go if you want to enjoy a well-hung steak served the British way, or, for those ready to take it on, the famous Mixed Guinea Grill itself. The restaurant is old school, with white tablecloths, wooden panel and discrete booths. Prices are typically a little higher than most gastropubs, reflecting the area and setting. The business is owned by pub operator Youngs, so there is a good choice of cask ales offered in the bar, as well as an excellent wine list. Head chef Mark Newbury focuses on British classics from long-established suppliers, including London-cure Scottish smoked salmon, and beef from Godfrey's butchers, which has a dry-aging room dedicated to the Guinea.

Il faut savoir que la guinée, équivalente à une livre et un shilling, était l'unité monétaire préférée des gentlemen. Et si le Guinea Grill a ouvert à Mayfair, près de Berkeley Square, en 1952, existe ici une auberge depuis 1423. C'est surtout l'adresse à recommander pour se régaler d'une pièce de bœuf de qualité et maturée à la façon britannique, ou, pour ceux qui sont de taille, du fameux Mixed Grill version Guinea. La salle joue à merveille la tradition, nappes blanches, lambris et alcôves discrètes. Les prix, plus élevés que dans la plupart des gastropubs, suivent cependant ceux du quartier. Le chef Mark Newberry travaille les produits classiques et sait s'approvisionner auprès de fournisseurs bien établis, saumon fumé d'Écosse London Cure ou bœuf des boucheries Godfreys qui, d'ailleurs, possèdent une chambre de maturation réservée au Guinea. Cet établissement appartenant à Youngs, on y trouve sans surprise une bonne sélection de bières de fût au bar ainsi qu'une belle carte des vins.

À la carte : Classic prawn cocktail with marie rose sauce / *Cocktail de crevettes classique à la sauce marie rose* 9,50 £ • London cure,

scottish smoked salmon and caper berries / *Saumon fumé écossais London Cure et câpres* 13,50 £ • Sticky toffee pudding with clotted cream / *Sticky toffee pudding et crème épaisse* 6,10 £.
Closed Sundays / *Fermé le dimanche*

🍲 HEREFORD ROAD RESTAURANT

🍲 3 Hereford Road, Westbourne Grove, London, W2 4AB
Tube / *Métro* : Bayswater (Circle/District)
+44 20 7727 1144
www.herefordroad.org

Located in the Notting Hill Gate area, Hereford Road occupies a site that was a butcher's shop in Victorian times, and sets out to be a neighbourhood restaurant championing British food at prices which reflect seasonal availability. The driving force is chef and co-founder Tom Pemberton previously head chef at St. John Smithfield. The shop front entrance leads to a white tiled counter, with an open kitchen on show, reflecting the artisan approach. Diners on the ground floor can sit in booths to watch the food being prepared, while the downstairs dining area can seat larger groups. The menu is a meat-eater's delight, with interesting and unusual cuts of meat and game, as well as fresh fish, simply paired with seasonal produce. Larger cuts are offered as sharing options, and good value wines are available to accompany the food.

Ce pub est installé à l'emplacement qu'occupait à l'époque victorienne un boucher. Il se veut restaurant de quartier comme défenseur d'une cuisine britannique et accessible car travaillant les produits de saison. Tom Pemberton, chef, co-fondateur et ancien chef du St. John Smithfield, en est le fer de lance. L'entrée, façon boutique, donne sur un comptoir à carreaux blancs, avec une cuisine ouverte qui atteste bien de cette approche artisanale. Au rez-de-chaussée, les convives peuvent s'asseoir dans des alcôves et regarder les plats se préparer, alors qu'au sous-sol, l'espace est plutôt réservé aux groupes. La carte fait le bonheur des carnivores, avec viandes ou gibiers toujours bienvenus et souvent méconnus, tout en comprenant aussi des poissons frais qu'accompagnent le plus simplement des légumes de saison. On recommandera les grosses pièces de viande destinées à être partagées, et on se fera plaisir avec les vins d'un bon rapport qualité prix.

À la carte : Ham hock, white cabbage and chervil / *Jambonneau, chou blanc et cerfeuil* 7 £ • Lamb's sweetbreads, green beans and toasted barley / *Ris d'agneau, haricots verts et orge grillé* 7,90 £ • Whole lemon sole, tomato and sea dulse / *Limande sole entière, tomate et dulse de mer* 16,50 £ • Bakewell tart / *Tarte Bakewell* 6 £.
Open every day / *Ouvert tous les jours*

🍽 LADY OTTOLINE
🍽 11a Northington Street, WC1N 2JF
🍽 Tube / *Métro :* Chancery Lane (Central)
+44 20 7831 000820 7831 0008020 7831 0008
www.theladyottoline.com

Bloomsbury has long been populated by London's literary and artistic, and the Lady Ottoline reflects this both inside and out. The pub is named for Lady Ottoline Morrel, an aristocratic patron – and lover – of many renowned writers and artists. From the elegant street corner pub exterior, the door opens onto a long, dark wood bar and a mixed wood and tile floor. An interesting and eclectic collection of artwork adorns the walls. Diners are welcome to eat in the main bar, which has a range of draught beers worth exploring with a pork pie or scotch egg from the bar menu, or a full meal. Tables can be booked in the upstairs dining room, with a private dining option also available. The menu offers a welcome choice of comforting British dishes with a fresh and seasonal twist, overseen by head chef Greg Martin, accompanied by a well-chosen wine list.

Bloomsbury est depuis longtemps le quartier de prédilection de la scène littéraire et artistique londonienne, le Lady Ottoline en étant un bel exemple. Il tire son nom de Lady Ottoline, aristocrate mécène et amante de nombreux écrivains et artistes célèbres. La porte de ce pub aux extérieurs élégants, s'ouvre sur un long bar sombre et sur un sol de carrelage et de bois. Une collection d'art originale et éclectique orne les murs. Les clients aiment s'installer au comptoir et apprécier la sélection de bières pression qu'accompagnent si bien tourtes au porc ou Scotch eggs de la carte, comme le menu. Ils peuvent aussi réserver une table à l'étage, voire en privatiser une partie. La carte, supervisée par le chef Greg Martin, propose un choix intéressant de plats britanniques toujours rassurants, à la touche fraîche et de saison. Sélection de vins bien choisie.

À la carte : Hand-picked cornish crab, pickled cucumber, sourdough toast / *Crabe de Cornouaille décortiqué à la main, concombre au vinaigre, pain au levain grillé* 9,50 £ • Chicken liver parfait, madeira, piccalilli / *Parfait de foies de volaille, madère, condiment Piccalilli* 7 £ • Dingley dell pork loin, butter beans, chorizo, salsa verde / *Longe de porc Dingley Dell, haricots beurre, chorizo, salsa verde* 18 £ • Baked vanilla cheesecake, Sicilian blood orange / *Cheesecake à la vanille, orange sanguine de Sicile* 6,50 £.
Closed Sunday evening / *Fermé le dimanche soir*

NORFOLK ARMS

28 Leigh St, London WC1H 9EP
Tube / *Métro :* Russell Square (Piccadilly)
+ 44 20 7388 3937
www.norfolkarms.co.uk

The West End is better served by branded restaurant groups than it is by good value independents, so the Norfolk Arms offer a welcome change. The pub is in a prominent street corner location close to Russell Square, and clearly communicates its gastropub credentials by hangings delicacies such as ham and strings of onions in the window. The menu offers a wide choice of British dishes, using fresh and seasonal ingredients, but what singles out the Norfolk Arm is its choice of around 40 tapas dishes, both British and Spanish, which are ideal for groups of friends wanting to share a lively and interesting meal featuring an array of fresh and interesting flavours, all cooked to order.

Dans ce West End plus réputé pour ses restaurants de chaînes que ses adresses de qualité, bienvenue au Norfolk Arms ! Situé dans une rue réputée et proche de Russell Square, les jambons ou chapelets d'oignons accrochés aux fenêtres apportent bien la preuve que ce Norfolk Arms est de la race des gastropubs... À la carte, un large choix de plats britanniques, tous préparés avec de bons produits de saison. Mais ce qui fait l'originalité et l'intérêt de l'adresse, c'est la quarantaine de tapas proposée, au registre aussi bien britannique qu'espagnol, tous préparés à la commande, et qui, autour de saveurs percutantes et variées, font le bonheur des repas entre amis.

À la carte : Lyme bay dorset crab with rocket, ginger, chilli, honey, soy and sesame dressing / *Crabe de la baie de Lyme dans le Dorset, roquette, gingembre, piment, miel, soja et sésame* 9,50 £ • Scotch egg, mustard (tapas) / *Scotch egg, moutarde* 5 £ • Serrano ham croquettes, caramelised red onion (tapas) / *Croquettes de jambon Serrano, oignon rouge caramélisé* 5,50 £ • Whole sea bream with sauteed spinach and raisins, madeira sauce / *Dorade entière, épinards sautés aux raisins secs, sauce au madère* 15,50 £ • Coffee pannacotta with whisky cream and roasted almond / *Panna cotta au café, crème au whisky et amandes rôties* 4,50 £.
Open every day / *Ouvert tous les jours*

POLPO AT APE & BIRD

142 Shaftesbury Avenue, London WC2H 8HJ
Tube / *Métro :* Leicester Square (Northern/Piccadilly)
+44 20 7836 3119
www.apeandbird.com

Polpo is a group of Venetian bistros in some of London's more upmarket areas, and with the Ape & Bird restaurateur Russell Norman has brought the same small plate approach to the heart of one of London's busiest areas. The pub, close to Leicester Square and formerly known as the Marquis of Granby, has been redesigned to include a basement bar, ground floor pub, and first floor restaurant, all with a different feel. The menu features a wide selection of freshly cooked, tempting small plate Venetian-style specialities with the occasional London twist. Diners are encouraged to share, and order as wide a selection as possible. Reflecting its West End location, Polpo at Ape & Bird has a lively feel, making it an ideal venue to enjoy a meal with a group of friends.

Polpo, c'est le nom d'un groupe de bistrots vénitiens situés dans les quartiers huppés de Londres. Ape & Bird, c'est l'œuvre du restaurateur Russell Norman qui a apporté ce concept de petites assiettes au cœur d'un des quartiers les plus animés de Londres. L'adresse, proche de Leicester Square et connue avant sous le nom de Marquis of Granby, a été transformée pour loger un bar au sous-sol, un pub au rez-de-chaussée et un restaurant au premier étage, chaque espace revendiquant sa propre ambiance. Sur la carte, des petites assiettes donc, toutes appétissantes, fraîchement cuisinées, et défendant un style évidemment vénitien, avec de temps en temps une touche londonienne. On prend d'ailleurs ici plaisir à partager comme à commander le maximum de recettes parmi un large choix. Voilà donc un bistrot qui colle bien à l'ambiance du quartier du West-End, animée et joyeuse, et qui est à connaître pour se régaler entre amis.

À la carte : Potato and parmesan crocchette / *Croquette de pommes de terre au parmesan* 4 £ • Chopped chicken liver crostini / *Crostini aux foies de volaille* 4 £ • Rustego, chestnut mushroom and ricotta pizzette / *Pizzette aux pleurotes et ricotta* 8 £ • Flourless chocolate and hazelnut cake / *Gâteau sans farine au chocolat et noisette* 6 £.
Open every day / *Ouvert tous les jours*

🍵 THE PUNCHBOWL
🍵 41 Farm Street, Mayfair, London, W1J 5RP
Tube / *Métro :* Green Park (Victoria/Jubilee)
+ 44 207 493 6841
www.punchbowllondon.com

....

The Punchbowl has been part of the social scene in London's upmarket Mayfair district since 1729, and both outside and in is everything visitors to London expect from a proper English tavern. Its more recent history is just as interesting, with film director Guy Ritchie having owned the pub for several years, and his then-wife Madonna famously extolling the virtues of a pint of Timothy Taylor Landlord bitter. Since 2013, the pub has been owned by the Cirrus Inns business of gastropub entrepreneur Alex Langlands Pearse. Diners after a quick bite might want to try the excellent bar snacks accompanied by a pint of cask ale or a single malt whisky. There is also a pub menu, featuring classic dishes such as fish & chips and the house pie, as well as the main restaurant menu which offers British specialities with a strong focus on seasonality.

Depuis 1729, le Punchbowl fait partie de la vie de Mayfair, quartier huppé s'il en est. Il a tout pour plaire aux visiteurs qui, de passage à Londres, souhaitent découvrir une authentique taverne à l'anglaise. Son passé récent ne manque pas non plus d'intérêt : propriété du réalisateur Guy Ritchie pendant quelques années, Madonna, son épouse d'alors, y a fait la promotion de la bière Timothy Taylor Landlord. Depuis 2013, le pub a rejoint le groupe Cirrus Inns, qui gère des gastropubs et appartient à Alex Langlands Pearse. Si le pub dispose d'une carte aux plats classiques, fish and chips ou tourte maison notamment, on se laissera volontiers tenter par les excellents en-cas, en les savourant pourquoi pas accompagnés d'une pinte de bière de fût ou d'un whisky single malt. Au restaurant principal, l'accent est surtout mis sur les spécialités britanniques et les produits de saison

À la carte : Ham hock, piccalilli, and sour dough / *Jambonneau, condiment Piccalilli et pain au levain* 7,50 £ • Hand dived scottish scallops, apple, bacon and butterscotch / *Saint-jacques écossaises pêchées à la main, pomme, bacon et butterscotch* 12,50 £ • The Punchbowl pie with seasonal vegetables (pub menu) / *Tourte Punchbowl aux légumes de saison* 15,50 £ • Pan-fried whole lemon sole, spinach, new potatoes, caper and brown shrimp butter / *Limande sole entière poêlée, épinards, pommes de terre nouvelles, câpres et beurre de crevette* 20,50 £ • Rhubarb and apple crumble with devon cream / *Crumble pommes rhubarbe, crème du Devon* 7,50 £.
Open every day / *Ouvert tous les jours*

🍵 THE SCARSDALE TAVERN

23a Edwardes Square London W8 6HE
Tube / *Métro :* High Street Kensington (Circle, District)
+ 44 20 7937 1811
www.scarsdaletavern.co.uk

The striking front terrace garden, with its lovingly tended flower baskets and tubs, makes the Scarsdale one of Kensington's more visually appealing pubs. Located on an upmarket residential square close to High Street Kensington, the Scarsdale boasts more millionaires in the bar than most pubs given local property prices. Since buying the pub in 2009, Fuller's Brewery has transformed the menu, investing in an open kitchen and putting the focus on freshly cooked, high quality ingredients including the delicious signature shoulder of lamb. There's an emphasis on pub food classics such as the pie of the day, matched to a Fuller's beer, and the front bar is an ideal pace to enjoy freshly cooked bar food including steak sandwiches and burgers, accompanied by a pint.

Avec sa terrasse, ses paniers et bacs à fleurs amoureusement entretenus, le Scarsdale est certainement l'un des plus jolis pubs de Kensington. Situé dans un square huppé à proximité de High Street Kensington, il peut aussi s'enorgueillir d'accueillir à son bar la plus grande concentration de millionnaires eu égard aux prix de l'immobilier des environs... Le brasseur Fuller's, propriétaire depuis 2009, a changé la carte, investi dans une cuisine ouverte et privilégié des produits de première qualité et fraîcheur comme la délicieuse épaule d'agneau devenue plat-signature de la maison. On y retrouve tous les grands classiques du registre bistrotier, tourte du jour notamment à accompagner d'une bière Fuller's. Au comptoir, on se régale tout autant d'un repas léger et fraîchement préparé, sandwichs à la viande ou burgers arrosés d'une pinte notamment.

À la carte : Smoked salmon and asparagus fishcake, hollandaise sauce, mixed leaves / *Galette au saumon fumé et asperges, sauce hollandaise, mesclun* 8,50 £ • Grilled goats cheese salad with red onion marmalade / *Salade au chèvre chaud, confiture d'oignons rouges* 8,50 £ • Cumberland sausages with herb mash and onion gravy / *Saucisses du Cumberland, purée aux herbes et jus à l'oignon* 11,25 £ • Eton Mess / *Eton mess* 6,95 £.
Open every day / *Ouvert tous les jours*

🍽 TRUSCOTT ARMS
🍽 55 Shirland Rd London W9 2JD
🍽 Tube / *Métro* : Warwick Avenue
+44 20 7266 9198
www.thetruscottarms.com

Located in West London not far from Paddington, the Truscott Arms is an imposing Victorian pub, lovingly refurbished and offering a choice of bars and dining on three floors. Head chef Aidan McGee, who took over the kitchen in September 2014, has previously worked at Michelin-starred restaurants and has continued to develop the pub's reputation for imaginative modern dishes using locally sourced ingredients and seasonal produce. The focus on local food, as well as ensuing the menu offers choices such as gluten-free food, has earnt the pub the Sustainable Restaurant Association's highest accolade, Three Star Sustainability Champion. For those looking to enjoy a traditional Sunday lunch, the Truscott Arms won the Best British Roast Dinner award in 2014. The dining menu is available in the garden during the summer.

À l'ouest de Londres, non loin de Paddington, le Truscott Arms est un pub victorien qui en impose, car rénové avec amour et proposant sur trois étages bars ou salles à manger. Le chef Aidan McGee en a repris les fourneaux en septembre 2014, après avoir travaillé dans des restaurants étoilés. Il perpétue la réputation de l'endroit : cuisine créative et contemporaine, confectionnée à base de produits saisonniers provenant des environs. Cette défense d'une cuisine locale comme la mise à la carte de plats sans gluten, ont permis au pub d'obtenir la plus importante distinction du Sustainable Restaurant Association's (l'association des restaurants durables). Et pour ceux qui ont envie d'un déjeuner dominical traditionnel, qu'ils se réjouissent, le Truscott Arms a également gagné en 2014 le prix du meilleur rôti ! Bon à savoir, pendant l'été, les plats de la carte sont servis dans le jardin.

À la carte : Scottish scallops, smoked bacon, peas, lemon, truffle / *Saint-jacques écossaises, bacon fumé, petits pois, citron, truffe* • Veal sweetbreads, lavender honey, hazelnuts, endive / *Ris de veau, miel de lavande, noisettes, endive* • South downs lamb (neck and tongue) with baby leeks, broad beans, potatoes, heirloom tomatoes / *Agneau de South Downs (collier et langue) avec*

poireaux crayon, fèves, pommes de terre et tomates anciennes ●
Red mullet, wild garlic, Jersey royals, rainbow chard, Wiston
Estate wine and grapes / *Rouget, ail sauvage, pommes de terre
Jersey Royals, blettes arc-en-ciel, sauce au vin Wiston Estate et
aux raisins.*
Closed Mondays and Tuesdays / *Fermé le lundi et le mardi*

South London

🍲 THE ADMIRAL CODRINGTON
🍲 17 Mossop Street, London SW3 2LY
Tube / *Métro :* Sloane Square (Circle/District)
+ 44 20 7581 0005
www.theadmiralcodrington.co.uk

....

Located in the ever-fashionable Kensington/Knightsbridge area, the Admiral Codrington is one of London's most acclaimed dining pubs, attracting a much broader customer base than most pubs and wine bars in the area thanks to its high quality food. The main bar has a traditional feel, while the adjacent restaurant is bright and modern. Meat, and especially beef, is a speciality of the 'Ad Cod', as locals call it. The juicy house burger often appears on lists of London's best, and the pub's Wednesday Burger Night features special limited range burgers in unusual and interesting flavour combinations. For bigger appetites, rare breed beef is available in sizes up to a 1000g rib of 30 day aged beef for two to share. It's also definitely worth leaving room for the delicious home-made desserts. The Admiral Codrington is part of the Cirrus Inns gastropub group.

Ce pub, parmi les plus renommés de Londres, attire dans le quartier toujours à la mode de Kensington/Knightsbridge, une clientèle qui n'hésite pas à venir de loin pour la qualité de sa cuisine. Le bar principal reste fidèle à son ambiance traditionnelle quand le restaurant adjacent se montre plus lumineux et contemporain. La viande, et plus particulièrement le bœuf, est une des spécialités du « Ad Cod », comme aiment l'appeler les habitués. Sachez que le burger maison est souvent cité parmi les meilleurs de Londres et que la soirée burgers du mercredi propose des compositions aux saveurs aussi originales que surprenantes. En cas de grosse faim, du bœuf issu de races rares est proposé, avec des côtes d'un kilo pour deux et maturées trente jours ! N'oubliez cependant pas de garder de la place pour les desserts, tous faits maison.

À la carte : Salt and pepper squid green chilli, spring onion, coriander, nuoc cham / *Calamar poivre et sel, piment vert, oignon frais, coriandre, nuoc cham* 8,50 £ • Ham hock terrine crumbled

walnut, prune and brandy purée / *Terrine de jambonneau, crumble de noix, purée de pruneaux au cognac* 6,75 £ • Sticky toffee pudding with vanilla ice cream / *Sticky toffee pudding, glace vanille* 6,75 £.
Open every day / *Ouvert tous les jours*

ANCHOR & HOPE
36 The Cut London SE1 8LP
Tube / *Métro* : Waterloo (Northern, Jubilee, Bakerloo)
+ 44 20 7928 9898
www.anchorandhopepub.co.uk

Opened in 2003, the Anchor & Hope is one of London's best known gastropubs, with its location close to Waterloo station putting it firmly on the map for both visitors and local workers and residents. Specialising in meat and game, along with traditional pub dishes, the Anchor & Hope does not take bookings except for Sunday lunch. This can make a visit challenging at busy times, but the delicious, freshly cooked food is worth the effort. Prospective diners are advised to arrive early in order to get on the list when the pub starts taking names for the 6pm dinner sitting from 5.15pm onwards. Later in the evening, if no tables are immediately available, the maitre d'hotel will estimate the waiting time and invite diners to have a drink or two in the bar. On warmer evenings, the menu is also served outside. At lunchtime, the pub offers a daily changing 'Workers Lunch' menu priced at £15.00 for two courses or £17.00 for three courses, which is usually served quickly.

Ouvert en 2003, l'Anchor & Hope est un des plus célèbres gastropubs de Londres. Proche de la gare de Waterloo, il est devenu le rendez-vous aussi bien des voyageurs que des travailleurs et habitants du quartier. Il a fait de la viande, du gibier et des plats traditionnels sa spécialité. Il ne prend pas de réservations, à l'exception du déjeuner du dimanche. Trouver une place aux heures de pointe n'est jamais une mince affaire, mais sa fraîche et délicieuse cuisine mérite bien un peu de patience ! Il est d'ailleurs toujours possible d'arriver vers 17h15, d'inscrire alors son nom pour espérer avoir une table dès le premier service de 18 heures. Plus tard dans la soirée, s'il n'y a pas de table disponible, le maître d'hôtel saura vous préciser le temps d'attente tout en vous invitant à boire un ou deux verres au bar. Et bon à savoir, les soirs de beau temps, les plats de la carte sont aussi servis dehors, et, à l'heure du déjeuner, un menu du jour est proposé et en général servi rapidement (compter 15£ pour deux plats ou 17£ pour trois).

À la carte : Beef consommé, madeira, fresh peas and tarragon / *Consommé de bœuf, madère, petits pois frais et estragon* 6,40 £ • Warm snail and bacon salad / *Salade tiède aux escargots et au bacon* 7,80 £ • Roast guinea fowl, gratin dauphinois, beet greens and asparagus / *Pintade rôtie, gratin dauphinois, fanes de betteraves et asperges* 16 £ • A grilled Orkney kipper and Jersey Royals / *Hareng fumé grillé d'Orkney, pommes de terre Jersey Royals* 11,80 £ • Muscat caramel custard / *Crème caramel au muscat* 6,40 £.
Closed Sunday evening / *Fermé le dimanche soir*

🍽 THE BALCON

🍽 Sofitel St James Hotel, 8 Pall Mall London SW1Y 5NG
Tube / *Métro :* Charing Cross (Bakerloo/Northern)
+44 20 7389 7820
www.thebalconlondon.com

The setting of the Balcon restaurant, located in the upmarket Sofitel St James Hotel at one of London's most prestigious addresses, definitely stretches the definition of the term 'bistro', but executive chef Vincent Ménage deserves respect and recognition for offering a complete rethink of the bland and overpriced fare most hotel restaurants offer. The brasserie-inspired menu includes a signature croque monsieur and a selection of small plates designed for a tapas-style mix-and-match approach. These dishes, along with the main menu, take inspiration from the best of British and French cuisine, using seasonal produce sourced from local suppliers. A note of caution for diners is that while the food is excellent value, the service and surroundings are very much restaurant rather than bistro quality. The price of wine and cocktails reflects the setting, so the drinks budget should be set accordingly.

Dans ce Sofitel Saint-James si chic et situé à l'une des adresses les plus prestigieuses de Londres, le cadre du restaurant Le Balcon ne correspond à l'évidence pas aux critères du bistrot... Le chef Vincent Ménage mérite pourtant respect et considération pour sa cuisine qui n'a décidément rien à voir avec celle trop souvent sans saveur et chèrement payée de la plupart des restaurants d'hôtels londoniens. Sur sa carte de style brasserie, le croque-monsieur signature comme la sélection de petites assiettes, genre tapas à partager, ne manquent ni d'intérêt ni de gourmandise. Comme tous les plats, ils prennent le meilleur de la cuisine britannique et française, et sont travaillés avec des produits de saison en direct de producteurs locaux. Et n'oubliez pas que, même si la carte affiche un excellent rapport qualité prix, le service et la salle restent bien ceux d'un restaurant... Quant aux prix des vins et des cocktails, ils suivent eux-aussi le standing du lieu, et mieux vaut se fixer un budget boissons en conséquence.

À la carte : Braised suckling pork cheek, parsnip puree, horseradish crumble (small plate) / *Joue de cochon de lait braisée, purée de panais, crumble au raifort* 7 £ • Gin marinated organic salmon, vegetables a la Grecque (small plate) / *Saumon bio mariné au gin, légumes à la grecque* 7 £ • Rhug farm organic chicken cocotte Grand Mere with bacon, mushrooms and potatoes / *Cocotte de poulet fermier bio grand-mère, bacon, champignons et pommes de terre* 19 £ • Wild sea trout fillet, Jersey Royal potatoes, seaweed butter and red pepper coulis / *Filet de truite de mer sauvage, pommes de terre Jersey Royals, beurre aux algues et coulis de poivron* 20 £ • English breakfast tea crème brulee and lemon madeleine / *Crème brûlée au thé English Breakfast et madeleine au citron* 5 £.
Open every day / Ouvert tous les jours

☕ THE BOOT & FLOGGER

10-20 Redcross Way, Southwark SE1 1TA
Tube / *Métro :* London Bridge (Northern/Jubilee)
+44 20 7407 1184
www.davy.co.uk

The Boot & Flogger near London Bridge is owned by the Davy family, who have been wine merchants in London for five generations, and takes its name from a traditional device used to put corks in wine bottles. The business

originally opened in 1965 in nearby Borough High Street, and relocated to its current side street address in 1973. Popular with traditional City types, the Boot & Flogger has a definite feel of the dining room of a traditional London gentleman's club. The menu reflects this, with a focus on traditional British dishes such as bangers & mash, although over the past year or so the Davy's Wine Bar group has updated its offer to include more salads and lighter dishes alongside the classics. The Boot & Flogger famously doesn't sell beer, instead offering an extensive list of Davy's wines by the glass and bottle. Other Davy's Wine Bars can be found at various London locations, see www.davy.co.uk.

Le Boot & Flogger près de London Bridge appartient à la famille Davy, marchands de vin à Londres depuis cinq générations, et tire son nom de l'outil traditionnel pour boucher les bouteilles de vin. À ses débuts en 1965, cet établissement était installé à Borough High Street avant de déménager à son adresse actuelle en 1973. Rendezvous prisé par la clientèle traditionnelle de la City, la salle à manger du Boot & Flogger sait cultiver l'ambiance d'un club privé pour gentlemen. Et pour preuve, la carte fait honneur aux plats britanniques traditionnels, saucisse purée notamment, même si depuis un an la maison Davy's l'a mise au goût du jour en ajoutant plus de salades et de plats légers... Bon à savoir, le Boot & Flogger ne vend pas de bières, préférant à l'évidence mettre en avant l'importante sélection de vins au verre et à la bouteille de la maison.

À la carte : Plate of smoked salmon / *Assiette de saumon fumé* 6,95 £ • Chicken liver pâté / *Pâté de foie de volaille* 6,95 £ • Bangers and mash with roasted red onion gravy / *Saucisses purée, jus à l'oignon rouge rôti* 11,95 £ • Grilled scallops and bacon with tiger prawns, spring onion and chilli / *Saint-jacques grillées, bacon, gambas tigrée, oignon frais et piment* 17,95 £.
Closed Sunday evening / *Fermé le dimanche soir*

🍺 THE BUTCHER'S HOOK

477 Fulham Road, SW6 1HL
Tube / *Métro* : Fulham Broadway (District)
+ 44 20 7385 4654
www.thebutchershook.co.uk

Diners will need to check the football fixtures before head-ing to the Butcher's Hook, since the pub's location opposite the Stamford Bridge stadium, home of Chelsea Football Club, means that is populated by enthusiastic football sup-porters enjoying pre and post-match beers when the team are at home. In fact, the building has a special place in sporting history as the site where the formation of the Chelsea club was agreed with a handshake. The menu changes frequently, with dishes featuring meat, fish and game according to seasonality, although diners can rely on 'landmarks' through the week such as BBQ night on Tuesdays and Steak Out Sundays, which offer fixed prices on a meal and a drink. All food on the menu comes with recommended matches from a well-chosen wine list. There is also a bar snack menu with dishes such as Welsh Rarebit and Duck Scotch Egg. A second Butcher's Hook has opened nearby at Ravenscourt Park.

Situé face au stade de Stamford Bridge qui abrite le Club de Chelsea, le Butcher's Hook est à éviter les jours où l'équipe joue à domicile et quand ses hordes de supporters s'adonnent à la bière avant comme après le match... Cette adresse occupe pourtant une place bien particulière dans l'histoire du sport, car c'est dans ce bâtiment qu'a été créé sur une simple poignée de main le club de Chelsea. La carte change souvent, avec ses plats de viande, de gibier ou de poisson qui suivent parfaitement les saisons. Mais les clients ont aussi ici leurs habitudes, comme la soirée barbecue du mardi ou les dimanches «Steak out», avec à chaque fois des formules «boissons comprises». Au menu, il est proposé d'intéressants accords mets et vins, la cave étant bien fournie. Et au bar est servie une sélection de plats rapides, Welsh Rarebit ou Scotch egg de canard no-tamment. À noter qu'un deuxième Butcher's Hook vient d'ouvrir au Ravenscourt Park voisin.

À la carte : Goat's cheese croquettes, rocket, fig compote / *Croquettes au fromage de chèvre, roquette, compote de figues* 6,95 £ • West Mersea rock oysters, shallot vinegar / *Huîtres*

de West Mersea, vinaigre à l'échalote 12 £ • Chargrilled côte de bœuf, chips, salad, peppercorn sauce / *Côte de bœuf à la braise, frites, salade, sauce au poivre vert* 25 £ • Pan-fried sea trout, crushed herb potatoes, fennel and orange salad / *Truite de mer poêlée, écrasée de pommes de terre aux herbes, salade de fenouil à l'orange* 15,95 £ • Hot chocolate fondant, pouring cream / *Fondant chaud au chocolat, crème liquide* 6,50 £.
Open every day /Ouvert tous les jours

THE CANTON ARMS

177 South Lambeth Road, London SW8 1XP
Tube / *Métro :* Stockwell (Victoria/Northern)
+ 44 20 7582 8710
www.cantonarms.com

Like its stablemate pub the Anchor & Hope at Waterloo, the Canton Arms doesn't take bookings, but for groups of diners looking for wonderful, freshly cooked British food and an enjoyable atmosphere, it's worth making the trip south to Stockwell. If there's no table available immediately, diners are advised how long the wait is likely to be and shown to the large, well-stocked bar, Once seated, diners are free to order individual dishes from the menu, but it's recommended that you look at the chalkboards first. These feature daily, generous dishes that are designed to be shared by groups of two or more. Even if there's no time for a full meal, a pint of excellent bitter and the Canton Arms' signature bar snack, the foie gras toastie, or toasted sandwich, will justify the trip.

Comme son pub cousin l'Anchor & Hope à Waterloo, le Canton Arms ne prend pas de réservations. Si vous recherchez une cuisine britannique préparée avec sérieux, à base de bons produits frais et servie dans un cadre chaleureux, n'hésitez pas à vous déplacer au sud jusqu'à Stockwell. Et si aucune table n'est encore disponible, on vous conduira au bar, bien alimenté, tout en vous précisant combien de temps il vous faudra patienter. Une fois assis, vous aurez tout le loisir de commander les plats de la carte, sans oublier de jeter un regard sur l'ardoise avec ses suggestions du jour, copieuses et à partager. Vous pouvez très bien aussi vous contenter au bar du sandwich toasté au foie gras – l'assiette signature – accompagné d'une bonne bière pression, il vaut à lui seul le détour !

À la carte : Smoked eel, cucumber, beetroots and horseradish / *Anguille fumée, concombre, betteraves et raifort* 8 £ • Pressed old spot pig's head and radishes / *Tête de cochon pressée Old Spot et radis* 7 £ • Chicken, smoked ham and wild garlic pie (for two) / *Tourte au poulet, au jambon fumé, et à l'ail sauvage (pour 2 pers.)* 30 £ • Cherry and almond tart / *Tarte amandine aux cerises* 6 £.
Closed Mondays / *Fermé le lundi*

🐚 HARWOOD ARMS
🐚 Walham Grove London SW6 1QP
🐚 Tube / *Métro :* Fulham Broadway (District)
+ 44 20 7386 1847
www.harwoodarms.com

London's only Michelin-starred pub at the time of writing, the Harwood Arms was just another back street local until the current management reinvented it as a gastropub in 2008. The owners include chef, game expert and beer lover Mike Robinson, who also owns the Pot Kiln pub in rural Berkshire, and the food at the Harwood reflects his passions. All the venison on the menu is shot by Robinson himself, and there is a strong focus on game and wild food, including fish. A set price menu is offered at lunch and dinner. The bar snack menu includes the acclaimed Harwood Arms scotch egg, and visitors should check out the range of draught beers and ciders, including cask ales, as well as bottled beers and ciders, and ask for advice on matching them to the daily menu.

Seul pub étoilé au Guide Michelin à la date de sortie de ce guide, le Harwood Arms n'était d'ailleurs qu'un simple pub de quartier jusqu'à ce qu'en 2008 ses propriétaires décident d'en faire un gastropub. Parmi ces derniers, Mike Robinson, à la fois chef, expert en venaison, amateur de bière et également propriétaire du Pot Kiln dans le Berkshire, a réussi à façonner la cuisine du Harwood à son image comme selon ses passions. La carte fait ainsi la part belle aux produits sauvages, gibier chassé par Robinson lui-même ou poisson. Menus proposés au déjeuner comme au dîner et, au bar, sélection de plats de comptoir dont le réputé Scotch egg. À noter aussi l'impressionnant choix de bières ou cidres pression, en fûts ou bouteilles. N'hésitez d'ailleurs pas à vous faire conseiller pour les associer avec les plats du jour.

À la carte : Berkshire wood pigeon faggots with Jerusalem artichoke and grapes / *Fagots de pigeon sauvage du Berkshire avec des topinambours et des raisins* • Cornish mackerel rollmop with cucumber, elderflower, gooseberry and frozen buttermilk / *Rollmops de maquereau de Cornouaille, avec du concombre, du sureau et du lait ribot congelé* • Roast rump of English Rose veal with mousseron mushrooms, mashed potato and garlic scape / *Quasi de veau English Rose rôti avec des mousserons, purée et tiges d'ail* • Fillet of Cornish sea bream with Jersey royals, cucumber and seaweed / *Filet de daurade de Cornouaille avec des pommes de terre Jersey Royals, du concombre et des algues* • Raspberry jam doughnuts with orange sugar and vanilla cream / *Beignets à la confiture de framboises avec du sucre à l'orange et de la crème à la vanille.*
Open every day / *Ouvert tous les jours*

☕ THE ENTERPRISE
☕ 35 Walton Street, London, SW3 2HU
Tube / *Métro* : South Kensington (Circle/District/Piccadilly)
+44 20 7584 3148
www.theenterprise.co.uk

....

Due to its South Kensington location, the Enterprise attracts a younger, professional and affluent clientele, with dark wood and leather seats aiming to create the feel of a London member's club 'without the fee'. The menu prices also reflect the upmarket location, but the Enterprise is worth a visit to sample excellent gastropub food, and the better value bar menu is also worth trying. The food is British with a definite continental flourish. Highlights of the menu include high quality Scottish Buccleuch Beef, traditionally served lamb cutlets, and fresh fish in season. The extensive wine list is headed up by some well-chosen and good value house recommendations, and there is also a good selection of beers.

Situé dans le quartier de South Kensington, l'Entreprise n'a pas de mal à attirer une clientèle de cadres, jeunes et aisés, qui apprécient l'atmosphère de ce club privé anglais avec bois sombre et banquettes en cuir... sans en avoir à acquitter les frais d'admission. Les prix de la carte sont bien ceux d'un quartier huppé, mais l'adresse et son excellente cuisine de gastropub valent le détour. Au bar, la carte se montre plus abordable et mérite aussi de s'y intéresser. La registre est britannique, ce qui n'empêche pas quelques touches venues du continent. On recommandera le bœuf écossais de Buccleuch, les côtelettes d'agneau préparées de façon traditionnelle, comme le poisson qui suit les saisons. Imposante carte des vins avec des suggestions à la fois bien choisies et d'un bon rapport qualité prix, et sérieuse sélection de bières.

À la carte : Chicken liver parfait, toasted brioche / *Parfait de foies de volaille, brioche toastée* 8,75 £ • Grilled asparagus, smoked trout, dill hollandaise / *Asperges grillées, truite fumée, hollandaise à l'aneth* 9,25 £ • Herb crusted lamb cutlets, sauteed jersey royals, mint and broad bean salsa / *Côtelettes d'agneau en croûte d'herbes, pommes de terre Jersey Royals sautées, fèves et sauce à la menthe* 23,75 £ • Roast fillet of hake, braised baby gem, peas and courgette, wild garlic pesto / *Filet de merlu rôti, cœurs de sucrine braisés, petits pois et courgette, pesto à l'ail sauvage* 18,75 £ • Steamed ginger sponge pudding, banana and butterscotch ice cream, crème anglaise / *Pudding vapeur au gingembre, glace banane et butterscotch, crème anglaise* 7,50 £ • Apple tart tatin, cinnamon and honey ice cream / *Tarte tatin, glace miel et cannelle* 7,50 £.
Open every day / *Ouvert tous les jours*

☕ THE MALT HOUSE

☕ 17 Vanston Place, Fulham, London SW6 1AY
☕ Tube / *Métro :* Fulham Broadway (District)
  + 44 20 7084 6888
  www.malthousefulham.co.uk

Jolly Fine Restaurants, the business owned by Michelin-starred chef Claude Bosi, took over The Malt House in 2012, since when along with locals, the pub has been persuading more fashionable West London diners from nearby Chelsea and Knightsbridge to make the journey to Fulham Broadway. Prominently located on a large corner site, the Malt House dates back to 1729, and the business includes six hotel rooms. Alongside Chef's Specials featuring seasonal produce including game and fish, the menu celebrates

classic British pub food such as fish and chips, sausage and mash and burgers. The Malt house also has a charcoal BBQ grill producing succulent steaks which, weather permitting, can be enjoyed in the pub's courtyard garden. The bar snacks menu includes homemade Scotch Eggs to enjoy with a pint of Brakspear beer, while the pub is also renowned for its home-made Malted Vanilla Ice Cream.

Le chef étoilé Claude Bosi a repris le Malt House en 2012 via sa société Jolly Fine Restaurants et réussi à faire venir ici, en plus des habitués, la clientèle plus branchée de Knightsbridge ou Chelsea. Idéalement situé à un carrefour, le Malt House date de 1729 et dispose de six chambres. La carte ne se limite pas aux seules spécialités du chef, produits de saison, gibier ou poisson notamment, elle sait aussi défendre de traditionnelles recettes de pub bien britanniques, fish and chips, saucisses purée ou burgers. Le Malt House possède un barbecue, sur lequel sont préparés d'excellents steaks et qui, si le temps le permet, sont servis dans la cour-jardin. Enfin, parmi les plats de comptoir proposés au bar, le Scotch eggs maison est à déguster de préférence accompagné d'une bière Brakspear. À goûter également la glace vanille maltée qui participe à la réputation de la maison.

À la carte : Seared foie gras, pain d'epice, apple and pears / *Foie gras poêlé, pain d'épices, pommes et poires* 8,50 £ • Honey spiced duck terrine, date and almond chutney / *Terrine de canard au miel épicé, chutney de dattes et d'amandes* 7,50 £ • Rhug Estate venison, celeriac tagliatelle, pink fir potato, chocolate and orange jus / *Gibier de Rhug Estate, tagliatelles de céleri, pomme de terre Corne de Gatte, jus au chocolat et à l'orange* 19,50 £ • Oxford gold ale battered fish of the day, triple cooked chips and crushed peas / *Poisson pané du jour à l'Oxford Gold Ale, frites cuites trois fois, écrasée de petits pois* 13,50 £ • Malted ice cream, salted caramel, almond grue / *Glace maltée, caramel salé, grué d'amandes* 6,50 £.
Open every day / *Ouvert tous les jours*

🎩 THE PANTECHNICON ROOMS

🎩 10 Motcomb Street, SW1X 8LA
Tube / *Métro* : Hyde Park Corner (Piccadilly)
+44 20 7730 6074
www.thepantechnicon.com

In the heart of elegant Knightsbridge, the Pantechnicon Rooms is a pub and dining room named after the landmark 1830s building nearby, which was originally built as an art gallery. Set over four floors, the Pantechnicon offers diners a choice of carefully planned areas to enjoy a modern British menu with a focus on high quality meat served from the grill, including delicious dry-aged beef, rare breed pork, and memorable triple cooked chips as an accompaniment. The choice of fresh fish is also excellent, and all dishes can be matched with the venue's interesting wine. The ground floor bar is a great place for a casual meal with friends, with cask beers and cocktails also served. As well as with the more traditional first floor dining room, private dining rooms are also available. Part of the Cubitt House group of gastropubs.

Au cœur de l'élégant quartier de Knightsbridge, le Pentichon Rooms tire son nom du bâtiment voisin construit en 1830 et qui, à l'origine, était une galerie d'art. Ce restaurant et pub à la fois est installé sur quatre étages qui, organisés en différents espaces, permettent d'apprécier dans d'excellentes conditions la cuisine britannique contemporaine de la carte. Celle-ci met à l'honneur des viandes de qualité, délicieux bœuf vieilli à sec ou porc issu de races rares notamment, qu'accompagnent si bien des frites mémorables car cuites trois fois. Sans oublier la sélection de poissons d'une grande fraîcheur comme celle de vins pour des accords mets et vins réussis. Le bar du rez-de-chaussée ne manque pas non plus d'intérêt, parfait pour un repas décontracté entre amis, avec ses bières de fût et ses cocktails. Bon à savoir, en plus de la traditionnelle salle à manger du premier étage, possibilité de privatiser d'autres salles.

À la carte : Duck liver pâté, redcurrant jelly, pickles and ciabatta / *Pâté de foie de canard, gelée de groseille, cornichons et pain ciabatta* 9 £ • Scottish scallops, fennel, peas, chorizo dressing / *Saint-jacques écossaises, fenouil, petits pois, vinaigrette au chorizo* 10,50 £ • Gloucestershire old spot pork chop / *Côte de porc Old Spot du Gloucestershire* 18 £ • Fillet of sea bass, leeks, samphire, prosecco and mussel cream sauce / *Filet de bar, poireaux, salicorne, sauce à la crème au Prosecco et aux moules* 17 £ • Gooseberry and almond pie, lemon curd ice cream / *Tarte amandine aux groseilles à maquereau, glace au lemon curd 7 £.* **Open every day / *Ouvert tous les jours***

THE THOMAS CUBITT

44 Elizabeth Street, SW1W 9PA
Tube / *Métro* : Sloane Square (Circle/District)
+ 44 20 7730 6060
www.thethomascubitt.co.uk

Thomas Cubitt was London's leading master builder in the early 19th century and was responsible for planning much of the layout of fine houses and imposing squares in the Belgravia area, where the elegant pub that bears his name now stands. The Thomas Public House & Dining Rooms is a bright street corner building in what is still one of London's most fashionable areas for both dining out and shopping. The ground floor bar has many traditional features including an oak bar and the original oak floors. Downstairs the offer is upmarket pub food eaten at wooden tables, with the quality reflecting chef Phillip Wilson's passion for fresh, seasonal produce. In the upstairs restaurant the setting is more formal, which command higher prices, but the food quality, including succulent rare-breed pork, is far higher than many other restaurants in the area, and far better value, with a well-selected wine list.

Thomas Cubitt, architecte majeur du Londres du début du 19ème siècle, a aménagé une bonne partie de Belgravia, ses belles maisons et ses squares imposants. Et c'est dans ce quartier parmi les plus recherchés de Londres pour dîner ou faire du shopping, comme dans ce bâtiment lumineux de coins de rue, qu'est installé le pub qui porte son nom. Le bar du rez-de-chaussée a conservé une ambiance traditionnelle avec son comptoir comme son parquet d'origine en chêne. Au sous-sol, on sert sur des tables en bois une cuisine de pub plutôt haut de gamme qui se retrouve dans la passion du chef Phillip Wilson pour les bons produits de saison. À l'étage, le décor se fait plus solennel comme les prix plus élevés, tout en sachant que la qualité des plats servis, notamment le succulent porc de race, se situe bien au dessus de celle de bon nombre de restaurants du quartier. Heureuse sélection de vins.

À la carte : Lamb burger, caramelised onion, mint yoghurt, sweet potato chips and bacon mayonnaise / *Burger d'agneau, oignon caramélisé, yaourt à la menthe, frites de patate douce et mayonnaise au bacon* 14,50 £ • Middle White pork sausages, champ, tenderstem broccoli and Guinness gravy / *Saucisses de porc Middle White, champignons, brocoli, jus à la Guinness* 18 £ • Smoked quail, new season baby beets, Scotch egg, charred endive / *Caille fumée, jeune betteraves de saison, Scotch egg, endive cuite à la braise* 9,50 £ • Pan fried john dory, Jersey Royals, smoked brown shrimps, chive cream sauce / *Saint-pierre poêlé, pommes de terre Jersey Royals, crevettes fumées, sauce à la crème et ciboulette* 21,50 £ • Peach, custard brioche, raspberry ice cream / *Brioche, crème anglaise à la pêche, glace à la framboise* 7,50 £.
Open every day / *Ouvert tous les jours*

East London

🍲 BLIXEN
🍽 65A Brushfield Street, London E1 6AA
Tube / *Métro* : Liverpool Street (Central/ Circle)
+44 20 7101 0093
www.blixen.co.uk

....

Blixen sits at the entrance to Spitalfields Market, making it ideal for a meal after shopping for vintage records and clothing. If the weather's fine there is the chance to enjoy an al fresco craft beer, cocktail or an intriguingly-named smoothie, such as the 'End Strife', before dining in the leafy, shabby-chic conservatory at the back of the more formal restaurant and bar. Like sister brasserie the Riding House Café near Oxford Circus, Blixen's menus run from breakfast through to dinner, taking in brunch, lunch, 'middle ground' light meals and snacks on the way. The menu has a healthy feel, with tempting dishes featuring light and fresh ingredients such as beetroot hummus and a nutrient-packed kale, beetroot, avocado and pickled courgette salad, alongside more comforting favourites.

Située à l'entrée du marché de Spitalfields, voilà l'adresse idéale pour se restaurer après avoir chiné vinyles ou vêtements vintage. Si le temps s'y prête, on n'hésitera pas à se rafraîchir d'une bière artisanale, d'un cocktail ou d'un smoothie au nom parfois surprenant comme ce « Fin de conflit », avant d'aller dîner dans le jardin d'hiver, avec ses arbustes et son style « shabby chic », situé derrière les plus classiques bars et restaurants. Comme au Riding House Café, sa brasserie sœur d'Oxford Circus, la carte du Blixen va du petit-déjeuner au dîner, sans oublier brunch, déjeuner, repas sur le pouce ou simples en-cas. La cuisine se veut saine, avec des assiettes à la fois appétissantes et légères, comme ce houmous de betterave ou cette salade riche en nutriments à base de chou kale, betterave, avocat et courgettes au vinaigre, tout en proposant des plats au registre plus classique et réconfortant.

À la carte : Beetroot hummus and lavosh / *Houmous de bette-rave et pain lavash* 3,50 £ • Celeriac and black garlic soup with

cracked pepper brioche / *Soupe de céleri et ail noir, brioche au poivre concassé* 5 £ • Pistachio ice cream with lemon shortbread / *Glace à la pistache et sablé au citron* 6 £.
Open every day / *Ouvert tous les jours*

🍲 BRAWN
🍲 49 Columbia Rd, Bethnal Green E2 7RG
🍲 Tube / *Métro* : Bethnal Green (Central)
+ 44 20 7729 5692
www.brawn.co

Located in the increasingly upmarket East End, Brawn has made the most of the former furniture makers it occupies. There is a bright, open feel to the main dining area, as well as a back room which doubles as a location for private parties. The brickwork walls spotlight the work of local artists, helping to reinforce the neighbourhood bistro feel. The daily changing menu created by chef Ed Wilson features beautifully cooked traditional British dishes with a French twist, as well as imported charcuterie, and is sourced mainly through local producers and suppliers, A small plate selection gives diners the opportunity to taste more of the range of flavours on offer. The wine list reflects the passion of vintner Eric Narioo, a partner in Brawn, for bio-dynamic and natural wines. Brawn's owners also run the Terroirs wine bar in Charing Cross.

Dans le quartier de plus en plus huppé de l'East End, Brawn a réussi à tirer le meilleur parti de l'ancienne fabrique de meubles qu'il occupe. La salle à manger principale ne manque ni de lumière ni d'espace, d'autant qu'elle se prolonge d'une autre salle qui peut être également louée pour des soirées privées. Sur les murs de briques, des œuvres d'artistes locaux ont été accrochées, jusqu'à faire du Brawn le rendez-vous du quartier. La carte, conçue par le chef Ed Wilson et faisant la part belle aux producteurs ou fournisseurs locaux, change tous les jours. Elle propose des plats britanniques traditionnels, toujours parfaitement cuisinés, et auxquels la petite touche française ou les charcuteries importées apportent leur grain de sel.... On apprécie aussi les nombreux plats proposés en petites portions qui permettent de goûter à toutes ces saveurs. Quant à la cave, riche en vins naturels ou bio, elle reflète

*bien la passion d'Éric Narioo, un des associés de Brawn,
pour ce type de vins. Bon à savoir, les propriétaires de
Brawn gèrent aussi le bar à vins Terroirs à Charing Cross.*

À la carte : Red mullet, tomato, olive and basil / *Rouget, tomate,
olive et basilic* 9 £ • Chargrilled duck hearts, chickpeas, sumac
and pomegranate / *Cœurs de canard à la braise, pois chiches,
sumac et grenade* 7,75 £ • Wild rabbit tagliatelle / *Tagliatelles au
lapin de garenne* 13,75 £ • Cremet nantais, strawberries, pista-
chio / *Crémet nantais, fraises, pistaches* 7 £.
Closed Sunday evening / *Fermé le dimanche soir*

🐄 THE COW

4 Chestnut Plaza, Montfichet Road, London E20 1GL
Tube / *Métro :* Stratford (Central/Jubilee/DLR)
+44 20 8291 8644
www.geronimo-inns.co.uk/london-the-cow

A shopping mall might not be the obvious place to find
a gastropub, but Geronimo Inns seized the opportunity to
make London's pub food culture part of the experience for
visitors to the 2012 Olympics by opening the Cow within
the Westfield centre at the entrance to the Olympic Park
in Stratford. Part of the centre's extensive choice of res-
taurants, the Cow offers indoor and outdoor eating with a
menu that features regularly changing seasonal dishes and
pub food classics, including a small plate selection, while
the choice of bar snacks includes giant pork scratchings. A
BBQ menu is also offered, and the cask ale range is worth
exploring. A second site, the Bull, operates along very simi-
lar lines at the Westfield centre in Shepherds Bush in West
London.

*Un centre commercial n'est pas forcément l'endroit où s'at-
tendre à trouver un gastropub ! En ouvrant cette adresse
dans le centre Westfield, à l'entrée du parc olympique de
Stratford, le groupe Geronimo Inns a souhaité faire dé-
couvrir la cuisine des pubs de Londres aux visiteurs des
Jeux Olympiques de 2012. Et dans ce centre bien pourvu
en restaurants, le Cow permet de prendre ses repas à l'in-
térieur comme à l'extérieur, de profiter d'une carte qui
change souvent, de choisir entre recettes de saison ou*

*traditionnelles, en plus ou moins petites portions et, au
bar de goûter à des grattons de porc géants. Le Cow dispose
également d'une carte réservée au barbecue, comme d'une
sélection de bières de fût qui méritent d'être goûtées.*

À la carte : Soup of the day with crusty bread / *Soupe du jour et
pain de campagne* 5 £ • Rabbit and pork terrine, pear chutney,
toast / *Terrine de lapin et porc, chutney à la poire, pain grillé*
6,50 £ • Lamb leg steak, minted new potatoes / *Gigot d'agneau,
pommes de terre nouvelles à la menthe* 15 £ • Fish & Chips - sus-
tainable haddock, garden peas, chips, tartare sauce / *Fish and
chips : haddock de pêche durable, petits pois frais, frites et sauce
tartare* 11,95 £ • White chocolate and orange crème brulee /
Crème brûlée au chocolat blanc et à l'orange 3,50 £.
Open every day / *Ouvert tous les jours*

🍲 THE EAGLE

🍲 159 Farringdon Road, London EC1R 3AL
🍲 Tube / *Métro :* Farringdon (Circle/Metropolitan/
Hammersmith & City)
+ 44 20 7837 1353
www.theeaglefarringdon.co.uk

**The Eagle was created 25 years ago by budding restaura-
teurs Michael Belben and David Eyre who wanted to set up
their own venture, and the two are credited with coining
the term 'gastropub'. The Eagle takes its status as a proper
pub rather than a restaurant very seriously ; in general,
there are no bookings and the advice to diners is to come
early or late for the best chance of getting a table, and to
be prepared to share with other diners. Parties of six or
more can book a table, but only for the start of the serv-
ing period, 12.30pm for lunch and 6.30pm for dinner. The
day's menu is chalked on a blackboard above the bar, and
food is cooked to order in an open kitchen. This means an
occasional wait for food to be served, but it's all well worth
it for some of the best freshly cooked seasonal dishes and
daily available produce in London. Tapas style small plates
are delicious and a good value way to sample the range of
food the Eagle serves. A good range of draught and bottled
beers is available, along with a small but excellent value
chalkboard wine list.**

Cette adresse a été créée voici vingt-cinq ans par Michael Belben et David Eyre, deux restaurateurs qui débutaient et souhaitaient monter leur propre affaire. C'est désormais à eux qu'on attribue la paternité du terme gastropub. L'Eagle prend d'ailleurs très au sérieux sa dénomination de pub plutôt que de restaurant : ici pas de réservation - si les groupes à partir de six peuvent réserver, c'est seulement pour les débuts de service, à savoir 12h30 au déjeuner ou 18h30 au dîner - et il est conseillé d'arriver tôt ou au contraire tard pour espérer avoir une table et partager une telle expérience. L'ardoise avec ses plats du jour, vous la trouverez fixée au-dessus du bar, et c'est dans la cuisine ouverte que tous ces plats sont préparés à la commande. Aussi, vous devrez parfois vous armer de patience avant d'être servi, mais tout est ici réalisé à partir de produits frais du jour avec, à la clé, parmi les meilleures préparations de Londres. Quant aux petites portions, façon tapas et toutes délicieuses, elles permettent de goûter à cette cuisine sans trop se ruiner. Bonne sélection de bières pression et en bouteille, comme de vins à l'ardoise à l'excellent rapport qualité – prix.

À la carte : Beetroot risotto with caraway, gorgonzola and walnuts / *Risotto à la betterave, carvi, gorgonzola et noix* 8 £ • Linguini with mackerel and fennel, chilli, anchovy and parsley / *Linguines au maquereau et au fenouil, piment, anchois et persil* 9 £ • Piri-piri quail with giant cous-cous, pomegranate and tzatziki / *Caille au piri-piri avec de la semoule épaisse, grenade et tzatziki* 12 £ • Pan-fried whole lemon sole, beetroot greens and aioli / *Sole limande entière poêlée, fanes de betterave et aïoli* 13 £.
Closed Sunday evening / *Fermé le dimanche soir*

☕ THE FOX & ANCHOR

☕ 115 Charterhouse Street London EC1M 6AA
Tube / *Métro :* Barbican (Circle/Metropolitan/
Hammersmith & City)
+44 20 7250 1300
www.foxandanchor.com

....

Smithfield has been London's meat and livestock market for at least 800 years, and traditionally, pubs in the vicinity of the market were allowed to open at dawn to serve

the market's porters at the end of a night's work. The Fox & Anchor is an imposing Victorian pub, which still honours the tradition by opening at 7am from Monday to Fridays, and 8.30am at weekends, to serve a traditional full English breakfast to residents of its boutique hotel rooms, as well as to non-residents. The main lunch and dinner menu puts the focus on classic British food with, as you'd expect, plenty of rich meat dishes. The Fox & Anchor is well worth a lunchtime trip for its salt beef sandwich, served with chips and a pickle, or 'wally'. The business is owned by London operator Young's.

Depuis plus de 800 ans, Smithfield est le marché de viande et de bétail de Londres, obligeant les pubs des environs à ouvrir dès l'aube pour nourrir ceux qui y terminaient leur nuit de travail. Au Fox & Anchor, imposant pub victorien, on honore encore cette tradition, ouvrant dès 7 heures du lundi au vendredi et dès 8 heures 30 les week-ends, servant un petit déjeuner complet comme aiment le préparer les Anglais, et ce tant aux clients des chambres de son boutique-hôtel qu'à ceux de passage. La carte principale du déjeuner ou du dîner fait honneur aux classiques de la cuisine britannique avec, comme on peut s'y attendre, nombre de plats riches en viande. À midi, on recommandera le sandwich au bœuf salé, servi avec frites et cornichon. Propreté de l'opérateur londonien Young's.

À la carte : Cornish crab fritter, sweet corn puree and herb salad / *Croquette de crabe de Cornouaille, purée de maïs doux, salade d'herbes* 6,50 £ • Devilled chicken livers, toasted sourdough / *Foies de volailles à la diable, pain au levain grillé* 6,95 £ • Braised ox cheeks, blue cheese dumplings and baby veg / *Joues de bœuf braisées, boulettes de pain au bleu, jeunes légumes* 16,50 £ • Wild boar and apple bangers, mustard mash, apple sauce / *Saucisses de sanglier sauvage, purée à la moutarde, compote de pomme* 14,50 £ • Youngs' beer battered haddock, chips and mushy peas / *Haddock pané à la bière Young's, frites, écrasée de petits pois* 15,50 £ • Strawberry eton mess / *« Eton mess » à la fraise* 5,50 £. **Closed Sunday evening /** *Fermé le dimanche soir*

🍴 THE GUN
🍴 27 Coldharbour, London E14 9NS
🍴 Tube: Canary Wharf (Jubilee/DLR)
  +44 20 7515 5222
  www.thegundocklands.com

There has been a pub on the site of The Gun in the Docklands are for more than 250 years, with the name commemorating the cannon fired to celebrate the opening of the West India Docks in 1802. A fire destroyed much of the interior of the old building in 2001, and it was reopened by current owners and brothers Tom and Ed Martin in 2004 after a restoration project to restore the Grade II listed building in consultation with English Heritage. As a cornerstone of the Martin brothers' ETM Group of London gastropubs, The Gun has built a reputation for dishes made from local and seasonal British ingredients, as well as for the stunning view of the Thames from its riverside location. Head Chef Robert Hunter joined the business in June 2015 having worked for a number of hotels and restaurants across the world. Seasonal meat, fish and game, with British vegetables are a feature of the menu, as is homemade ice cream.

Depuis plus de 250 ans existe à cet endroit du quartier des Docklands un pub, son nom évoquant le coup de canon tiré pour célébrer l'ouverture des West India Docks en 1802. En 2001, un feu a détruit une grande partie de l'intérieur du bâtiment, pour, après un projet de restauration sous le contrôle du English Heritage (l'équivalent de nos Bâtiments Historiques), être réouvert en 2004 par les propriétaires actuels, Tom et Ed Martin. Vitrine du groupe de gastropubs des deux frères Martin, le Gun doit sa réputation à sa vue spectaculaire sur la Tamise, comme à sa cuisine à base de produits d'ici et bien de saison. Le chef Robert Hunter a rejoint l'affaire en juin 2015 après avoir œuvré dans de nombreux hôtels et restaurants de par le monde. La carte se distingue par ses viandes, poissons ou gibier de saison, tous accompagnés de légumes britanniques, comme par ses glaces faites maison.

À la carte : Wild rabbit, smoked chicken and black pudding terrine, piccalilli, toast / *Terrine de lapin de garenne, poulet fumé et boudin noir, condiment Piccalilli, pain grillé* 9,50 £ • Dressed dorset crab, lemon mayonnaise, melba toast / *Crabe du Dorset* décortiqué, mayonnaise au citron, toast Melba 15 £ • Wild suffolk fallow deer loin, braised shoulder, caramelised shallot, buttered kale, celeriac mousseline / *Longe de daim sauvage du Suffolk, épaule braisée, échalotes caramélisées, embeurrée de chou kale, mousseline de céleri* 24 £.

Open every day / *Ouvert tous les jours*

🦪 HIX OYSTER & CHOP HOUSE

🦪 36-37 Greenhill Rents, Cowcross Street, London, EC1M 6BN
🦪 Tube / *Métro* : Farringdon (Circle/Metropolitan/ Hammersmith & City)
+44 20 7017 1930
www.hixoysterandchophouse.co.uk

Chef Mark Hix has a number of London bars and restaurants, and Hix Oyster & Chop House is his modern take on London's traditional chop house venues, where City workers could buy a hearty lunch to set themselves up for an afternoon's banking. Situated close to Smithfield Market, London's historic meat market, the building was originally a sausage factory, with many original features remaining. With wooden floors, a marble oyster bar, tiled walls and white linen tablecloths, there's an air of combined elegance and utility. The choice of seasonal and daily changing dishes includes meats and steaks on the bone cooked to order, and oysters from around the British Isles. Pre and post theatre dinner bookings are available for the nearby Farringdon and Sadler's Wells venues.

Le Chef Mark Hix possède plusieurs bars et restaurants à Londres, et cette adresse est la version contemporaine du « chop house » traditionnel où les travailleurs de la City aimaient se restaurer d'un copieux déjeuner avant leur après-midi à la banque. Le bâtiment, à proximité de Smithfield Market, le marché de viande historique de Londres, était à l'origine une usine à saucisses et a conservé de nombreux éléments d'origine. Le parquet au sol, le bar à huîtres en marbre comme les nappes en lin blanc, confèrent au lieu une touche à la fois élégante et fonctionnelle. On trouve à la carte, qui change tous les jours, des plats de saison, avec viandes et steaks cuits sur l'os et à la demande, mais aussi des huîtres en provenance des îles britanniques. Bon à savoir, on peut réserver pour dîner avant ou après les spectacles des proches Farringdon ou Sadler's Wells.

À la carte : Launceston lambs sweetbreads with Lambridge farm peas and bacon / *Ris d'agneau de Launceston, petits pois de la ferme de Lambridge et bacon* 9,50 £ • De Beauvoir smoked salmon 'hix cure' with Corrigan's soda bread / *Saumon fumé De Beauvoir « Hix cure » avec pain « soda bread » de chez Corrigan's* 14,50 £ • Hanger steak with baked bone marrow / *Onglet, moelle cuite au four* 19,95 £ • Moyallon bacon chop with pink fir apple potato and green onion salad / *Côte de bacon Moyallon, salade de pommes de terre, pommes Pink Fir, et oignons verts* 21,50 £ • Cobrey farm rhubarb and apple pie / *Tarte rhubarbe et pommes de la ferme Cobrey* 7,25 £.
Open every day / *Ouvert tous les jours*

☕ THE JUGGED HARE

49 Chiswell Street, London, EC1Y 4SA
Tube: Barbican (Circle/Metropolitan/Hammersmith & City)
+ 44 20 7614 0134
www.thejuggedhare.com

The Jugged Hare was formerly a City drinking den on the corner of one London's biggest, but now closed, breweries. Close to the entrance of the Barbican arts centre, the front bar can be very busy before and after a play or concert. The pub is now owned by gastropub specialist ETM Group, who have given the large back room restaurant a traditional English ambience, with dark wood furniture and red leather booths. The theatre kitchen, including an eight-spit rotisserie and charcoal grill, is at the heart of a menu which includes spit-roast meats, seasonal British game, wild fish and shellfish, and there is always a pie of the day. Interesting wines are a speciality of the house, but diners can also respect the pub's history by choosing from a range of cask ales, including the house Jugged Hare Pale Ale, brewed across the river by Sambrook's brewery in Battersea. A pre-theatre menu is available from 5.30pm Monday to Saturday.

Cet ancien repaire des buveurs de la City, au coin d'une des plus importantes brasseries de Londres maintenant fermée et tout proche de l'entrée du Barbican Arts Centre, est très fréquenté avant et après théâtres ou concerts. Le groupe ETM, propriétaire de nombreux gastropubs, a su recréer dans cet espace une ambiance britannique bien traditionnelle, avec mobilier en bois sombre et alcôves en cuir rouge. La cuisine théâtrale, avec sa rôtisserie à huit broches et son gril au charbon, alimente la carte, viandes rôties à la broche, gibier britannique de saison, poissons sauvages, fruits de mer, sans oublier tourte du jour. Choix de vins toujours intéressant, à moins de préférer rester fidèle à l'endroit en dégustant des bières de fût, notamment la Jugged Hare Pale Ale, la bière maison brassée de l'autre côté de la rivière par Sambrook's à Battersea. Bon à savoir, un menu avant-théâtre est proposé à partir de 17h30 du lundi au samedi.

À la carte : Devilled lamb's kidneys on toast, red watercress / *Rognons d'agneau à la diable sur pain grillé, cresson rouge* 8,50 £ • Potted smoked mackerel, orange and fennel salad / *Verrine de maquereau fumé, salade fenouil et orange* 7,50 £ • Longhorn cheeseburger, chips / *Cheeseburger de Longhorn, frites* 16,50 £ • Slow roast Herdwick lamb shoulder for two diners, spring greens, Lyonnaise potatoes / *Épaule d'agneau de Herdwick confite (pour deux pers.) légumes de printemps, pommes de terre à la lyonnaise* 68 £ • Steamed banana cake, salted caramel, milk chocolate sorbet / *Gâteau vapeur à la banane, caramel salé, sorbet chocolat au lait* 6,50 £.
Open every day / *Ouvert tous les jours*

🍲 THE NARROW
🍲 44 Narrow Street London E14 8DP
Tube / *Métro :* Limehouse (DLR)
+ 44 20 7592 7950
www.gordonramsayrestaurants.com/the-narrow

Limehouse is part of the much transformed Docklands area of London, and has retained more of its original character than other areas, although its pubs now offer a typically warmer welcome to visitors than when their main customers were dock workers. Gordon Ramsay took over the Narrow almost a decade ago, and has turned the historic pub, once known as the Barley Mow, into a busy gastropub. The large outside terrace offers great views of the Thames, and there is an outdoor BBQ menu on summer weekends.

The menu features products from small British and European supplies, with a bar snacks menu which allows diners to sample a wider range of dishes. The bar area also offers an opportunity to relax by the river over cask beer, wine or even to share one of the Narrow's house cocktails.

Si Limehouse, quartier largement réhabilité des Docklands, a su mieux préserver son caractère d'origine que d'autres zones de Londres, il n'empêche, ses pubs se montrent particulièrement plus accueillants que lorsqu'ils étaient fréquentés autrefois par les dockers. Gordon Ramsay a repris le Narrow voici bientôt dix ans, transformant cette établissement historique autrefois connu sous le nom de Barley Mow, en un gastropub animé. Sur la grande terrasse avec vue sur la Tamise, un barbecue est servi les weekends d'été. La carte fait le plein de petits producteurs britanniques comme européens, et le bar a la bonne idée de proposer une sélection de bouchées pour apprécier le registre de la maison. Le bar est aussi l'endroit idéal pour se détendre au bord de la rivière en buvant bière de fût ou vin, voire en partageant une des spécialités de cocktails du Narrow.

À la carte : Potted salt beef with apple and potato bread / *Verrine de bœuf salé, pain à la pomme et pomme de terre* 8 £ • Smoked chicken with garlic croutons, baby gem and Caesar dressing / *Poulet fumé, croûtons à l'ail, cœurs de sucrine et sauce César* 9 £ • Barnsley lamb chop with broad beans, samphire and balsamic jus / *Côte d'agneau Barnsley, fèves, salicornes et jus au balsamique* 23 £ • Isle of mull salmon with mussels, crushed Jersey Royals and horseradish sauce / *Saumon de l'île de Mull, moules, écrasée de pommes de terre Jersey Royals et sauce au raifort* 16,50 £ • Granny smith apple mousse / *Mousse de pomme Granny Smith* 7 £.
Open every day / *Ouvert tous les jours*

POPPIE'S FISH & CHIPS
6-8 Hanbury Street, London, E1 6QR
Tube / *Métro* : Liverpool Street (Central, Circle, Metropolitan)
+44 20 7247 0892
www.poppiesfishandchips.co.uk

Located in Spitalfields in the heart of the City, Poppies has been serving authentic fish and chips since 1945 and was named the Best Independent Fish and Chip Restaurant in the UK in 2014. The restaurant recreates the feel of the 1940s and 1950s, with authentic memorabilia and a vintage jukebox. Fresh, sustainably caught fish is at the heart of the offer, with Poppies working with traders at London's local Billingsgate Market to get the best of the catch daily. As well as the traditional cod and haddock, fried in Poppies own recipe batter, diners can choose from a broader range of seasonal fish, such as plaice, sole and mackerel. Along with a small but well-chosen wine range, craft beers are also offered. Poppies has also now opened a second restaurant in Camden Town.

À Spitalfields, au cœur de la City, le Poppies sert d'authentiques fish and chips depuis 1945 et a reçu en 2014 le prix du « meilleur restaurant indépendant proposant des fish and chips de Grande-Bretagne ». L'ambiance est celle des années 40 ou 50 avec objets d'époque et jukebox vintage. Cet établissement a fait du poisson de pêche durable sa spécialité, et sait s'approvisionner auprès des fournisseurs du marché local de Billingsgate pour avoir le meilleur du jour. À côté des traditionnels cabillaud et haddock frits selon la recette maison, Poppies propose aussi une belle sélection de poissons de saison, plie, sole ou maquereau notamment. Petite carte des vins bien choisie et bières artisanales. Et, bon à savoir, une deuxième adresse a ouvert à Camden Town.

À la carte : Wholetail scampi / *Queues de gambas* 5,95 £ • Jellied eels / *Anguilles en gelée* 5,95 £ • Mackerel fillets and chips / *Filets de maquereau et frites* 11,90 £ • Large cod and chips / *Grand fish and chips de cabillaud* 14,90 £.
Open every day / *Ouvert tous les jours*

🍽 THE PRINCESS OF SHOREDITCH
🍽 76 Paul Street, London EC2A 4NE
Tube / *Métro :* Old Street (Northern)
Phone + 44 20 7729 9270
www.theprincessofshoreditch.com

Simplicity is the order of the day at the Princess of Shoreditch, a traditional East London street corner pub which has transformed itself into an acclaimed, award-winning dining destination. The food is locally sourced, very high quality, and cooked simply but imaginatively. The melt-in-the-mouth beef sourced from Chart Farm in Kent is the star of the menu, and the same farm also supplies venison and game birds in season. The lamb also comes from Kent, while pork is from the Highlands of Scotland and the fish changes according to the catch landed by day boats off the South West coast. The very well-chosen wine list is updated regularly, and the cask and craft beer range reflects the choice offered by the many small brewers that have set up shop in the Shoreditch area. The pub is owned by Noble Inns, with separate menus in the pub and dining room areas.

La simplicité est toujours à l'ordre du jour au Princess de Shoreditch, pub traditionnel d'un coin de rues de l'est de Londres et qui se veut une destination reconnue et appréciée. Les produits, tous de grande qualité, proviennent des environs et sont préparés avec simplicité et en même temps créativité. Le bœuf, délicieusement fondant de la ferme Chart du Kent, est la star de la carte, et c'est d'ailleurs cette même ferme qui fournit le gibier, notamment à plumes en saison. Quant à l'agneau, il est également originaire du Kent alors que le porc arrive des Highlands écossais et le poisson de petits bateaux de pêche de la côte sud-ouest. La carte des vins, toujours pointue, change régulièrement, et les bières artisanales font honneur aux nombreux petits brasseurs installés dans ce quartier de Shoreditch.

À la carte : Roasted quail, spiced pear purée, endive and watercress / *Caille rôtie, purée de poires épicée, endives et cresson* 8 £ • Confit pork belly, scallops, black pudding, pineapple jus / *Poitrine de porc confite, Saint-Jacques, boudin noir, jus à l'ananas* 19,50 £ • Poached hake, cornish new potatoes, lemon purée, courgette flowers / *Merlu poché, pommes de terre nouvelles de Cornouaille, purée de citron, fleurs de courgette* 16,50 £ • Chocolate financier, popcorn, salted caramel ice cream / *Financier au chocolat, popcorn, glace au caramel salé* 6,50 £.
Open every day / *Ouvert tous les jours*

🍽 ST JOHN SMITHFIELD

🍽 26 St. John Street London EC1M 4AY
🍽 Tube / *Métro :* Farringdon (Circle/Metropolitan/
Hammersmith & City)
+44 20 7251 0848
www.stjohngroup.uk.com

Close to London's centuries-old meat market at Smithfield, St John is one of the trailblazers of London's modern 'foody' businesses, and a pioneer of whole animal cooking, making the most of every cut. The building is a former smokehouse, which used to smoke ham and bacon from the market, and was in a sorry state before the St John team restored it and gave the outside its distinctive whitewashed appearance. Along with the restaurant, the business also includes a bakery and wine shop, while the daily changing bar snacks menu is worth a visit in its own right, offering dishes such as devilled kidneys and roast rarebit. Owners Fergus Henderson and Trevor Gulliver continue to diversify, with venues such as St. John Bread and Wine at Spitalfields and St John Maltby Street across the river near London Bridge, but Smithfield is where it all started.

Proche du plus que centenaire marché de viande de Smithfield, le St John a été parmi les premiers établissements à surfer sur le nouvel engouement des Londoniens pour la bonne chère. Il a été également le premier à cuisiner les viandes en entier et à tirer ainsi le meilleur de chaque morceau. Le bâtiment, qui servait autrefois à fumer jambon et bacon du marché, était en piteux état avant d'être restauré par l'équipe du St John qui a su lui donner cette blancheur extérieure si reconnaissable. En plus du restaurant, vous trouverez ici boulangerie et caviste. Quant au bar, sa sélection quotidienne de plats sur le pouce mérite à elle seule le détour, rognons à la diable ou rarebit rôti (sorte de croque-monsieur au cheddar) notamment. Les propriétaires Fergus Henderson et Trevor Gulliver continuent de se développer en ouvrant de nouvelles adresses à Spitalfields ou de l'autre côté de la rivière, près de London Bridge, tout en sachant que c'est à Smithfield que tout a commencé.

À la carte : Roast bone marrow and parsley salad / *Moelle de bœuf rôtie, salade de persil* 8,20 £ • Grilled ox heart, green beans and horseradish / *Cœur de bœuf grillé, haricots verts et raifort*

7,80 £ • Rabbit saddle and courgettes / *Quasi de lapin et courgettes* 18,60 £ • Lemon sole and tartar sauce / *Limande sole et sauce tartare* 18,90 £ • Bread pudding and butterscotch sauce / *Pudding au pain et sauce butterscotch* 8,40 £.
Closed Sunday evening / *Fermé le dimanche soir*

🍴 THE TOKEN HOUSE
4 Moorgate, London, EC2R 6DA
Tube / *Métro* : Moorgate
+44 20 7600 6569
www.tokenhousemoorgate.co.uk

The Token House, owned by Fuller's Brewery, is only open from Monday to Friday, reflecting its target market, those who work in the City. However, it's worth making the journey to Moorgate to try a menu of freshly-cooked American and French bistro style food, with a focus on high quality, fresh ingredients. Strategically located windows allow diners to see into the kitchen, with house specialities including steak tartare, chicken liver and foie gras parfait, spatchcock chicken to share, and Cobb salad. There is a Plats Du Jour menu which changes through the week. Various seating areas can accommodate smaller groups as well as the larger parties from nearby offices who use the pub for after-work drinks and meals. The Token House is also worth a visit for the impressive breakfasts, served from 8am Monday to Friday.

Cet établissement, propriété du brasseur Fuller's, n'est ouvert que du lundi au vendredi, callant ainsi ses horaires sur ceux d'une clientèle qui pour l'essentiel travaille à la City. Ce ne doit pas vous empêcher de venir jusqu'à Moorgate car le registre joue du bistrot français comme d'une fraîche cuisine version américaine, le tout à base de produits de grande qualité. Derrières les vitres bien placées des fourneaux, vous aurez tout le loisir de zieuter ce qui s'y passe, comme de découvrir les spécialités de la maison, steak tartare, parfait aux foies de volaille et au foie gras, poulet en crapaudine à partager, ou salade Cobb. Sans oublier la carte des plats du jour, qui change tout au long de la semaine. L'aménagement permet d'accueillir des groupes plus ou moins nombreux, et on vient volontiers ici après le travail boire un verre ou pendre un repas. À noter également, les petits-déjeuners impressionnants, servis à partir de 8 h du lundi au vendredi.

À la carte : London porter smoked salmon / *Saumon fumé London Porter* 7 £ • Steak tartare with fried quail egg and fries / *Steak tartare, œuf de caille frit et frites* 8,50 £ • Lemon tart / *Tarte au citron* 6 £.
Closed Saturdays and Sundays / *Fermé le samedi et le dimanche*

🍲 TRAMSHED

32 Rivington Street, London EC2A 3LX
Tube / *Métro :* Old Street (Northern)
+44 20 7749 0478
www.chickenandsteak.co.uk

Reflecting a trend for casual dining restaurants that specialise in doing just a few dishes very well, chef Mark Hix has demonstrated that it's possible to take the best ideas from the fast food sector and add just the right combination of quality and passion to create a memorable eating out experience. Tramshed focuses on chicken and steak, with sharing dishes a speciality, using Mighty Marble Himalayan salt dry-aged steak and free-range chicken from Swainson House Farm in Lancashire. As the name suggest the venue is a former tramshed, meaning the dining area can accommodate large parties, and also allowing room for a huge Damien Hirst formaldehyde sculpture of a cow and a cock. Starters and puddings change with the seasons. The basement CNB Gallery below the restaurant features the work of a range of artists.

Dans la mouvance de ces restaurants décontractés qui savent se cantonner à quelques plats bien exécutés, le chef Mark Hix réussit ici de mémorables dégustations en tirant le meilleur du registre propre aux fast foods, tout en y ajoutant qualité et passion. Tramshed a fait du poulet, élevé en plein air et en provenance de la ferme Swainson House dans le Lancashire, comme du bœuf, maturé et salé aux cristaux de sel de l'Himalaya, sa spécialité jusqu'à les proposer dans des assiettes à partager. Comme son nom l'évoque, le bâtiment accueillait un générateur pour tramways, ce qui laisse aujourd'hui assez de place pour installer une gigantesque sculpture au formol de Damien Hirst représentant une vache et un coq, comme pour accueillir des groupes importants. Les entrées et les desserts changent en fonction des saisons. Enfin, la galerie CNB au sous-sol présente les œuvres de plusieurs artistes.

À la carte : Beefballs 'McIlhenny' / *Boulettes de bœuf McIlhenny's* 5 £ • De Beauvoir smoked salmon 'Hix cure' with shaved fennel and pickled cucumber / *Saumon fumé De Beauvoir « Hix cure », avec lamelles de fenouil et concombre au vinaigre* 6,25 £ • Rib on the bone 1kg for 2-3 to share / *Côte de bœuf de 1 kg (pour 2 ou 3 pers.)* 65 £ • Ronnie's bramley apple pie / *Tourte aux pommes Bramley de Ronnie* 6,50 £.
Open every day / *Ouvert tous les jours*

LONDON

51 other good addresses /
51 autres bonnes adresses

NORTH

THE ALMA
59 Newington Green Road, London, N1 4QU
Tube / *Métro* : Highbury & Islington (Victoria)
+ 44 20 3620 7516

THE BOHEMIA
762-764 High Road N12 9QH
Tube / *Métro* : Woodside Park (Northern)
+ 44 20 8446 0294

THE DUKE OF CAMBRIDGE
30 St Peter's Street, Islington N1 8JT
Tube / *Métro* : Angel (Northern)
+44 20 7359 3066

THE HORSESHOE
28 Heath Street, Hampstead NW3 6TE
Tube / *Métro* : Hampstead (Northern)
+ 44 20 7431 7206

THE LION & UNICORN
42-44 Gaisford Street, Kentish Town NW5 2ED
Tube / *Métro* : Kentish Town (Northern)
+ 44 20 7267 2304

THE OLD BULL & BUSH
North End Way, Golders Green NW3 7HE
Tube / *Métro* : Golders Green (Northern)
+ 44 20 8905 5456

THE PRINCE
59 Kynaston Rd, London N16 0EB
Tube / *Métro* : Stoke Newington (Overground)
+ 44 20 7043 5210

THE SALT HOUSE
63 Abbey Road St John Wood NW8 0AE
Tube / *Métro* : St Johns Wood (Jubilee)
+ 44 20 7328 6626

THE SOMERS TOWN COFFEE HOUSE
60 Chalton St, NW1 1HS
Tube / *Métro* : Euston (Northern/Victoria)
+ 44 20 7387 7377

THE SPREAD EAGLE
141 Albert Street, Camden Town NW1 7NB
Tube / *Métro* : Camden Town (Northern)
+ 44 20 7267 1410

WEST

THE ANGLESEA ARMS
35 Wingate Road, Hammersmith, London, W6 0UR
Tube / *Métro* : Ravenscourt Park (Circle/District)
+ 44 20 8749 1291

BLUE BOAT
Distillery Wharf, Parr's Way W6 9GD
Tube / *Métro* : Hammersmith (Circle/District/Piccadilly)
+ 44 20 3092 2090

THE BOUNTIFUL COW
51 Eagle Street WC1 4AP
Tube / *Métro* : Holborn (Central/Piccadilly)
+ 44 20 7404 0200

DISTILLERS
64 Fulham Palace Road W6 9PH
Tube / *Métro* : Hammersmith (Circle/District/Piccadilly)
+ 44 20 8748 2834

DOCK KITCHEN
Portobello Dock
342–344 Ladbroke Grove Kensal Road W10 5BU
Tube / *Métro* : Kensal Green (Bakerloo)
+ 44 20 8962 1610

GREAT QUEEN STREET
32 Great Queen Street WC2B 5AA
Tube / *Métro* : Holborn (Central/Piccadilly)
+ 44 20 7242 0622

THE LADBROKE ARMS
54 Ladbroke Road Notting Hill Gate W11 3NW
Tube / *Métro* : Notting Hill Gate (Circle/District/Central)
+ 44 20 7727 6648

THE LAMB
94 Lambs Conduit Street, Bloomsbury WC1N 3LZ
Tube / *Métro* : Russell Square (Piccadilly)
+ 44 20 7405 0713

PARADISE BY WAY OF KENSAL GREEN
19 Kilburn Lane, Kensal Green W10 4AE
Tube / *Métro* : Kensal Green (Bakerloo)
+ 44 20 8969 0098

PRIX FIXE BRASSERIE
39 Dean Street W1D 4PU
Tube / *Métro* : Leicester Square (Northern/Piccadilly)
+ 44 20 7734 5976

ROCK & SOLE PLAICE
47 Endell St WC2H 9AJ
Tube / *Métro* : Covent Garden (Piccadilly)
+ 44 20 7836 3785

THE SHED
122 Palace Gardens Terrace W8 4RT
Tube / *Métro* : High Street Kensington (Circle/District)
+ 44 20 7229 4024

TERROIRS
5 William IV Street WC2N 4DW
Tube / *Métro* : Leicester Square (Northern/Piccadilly)
+ 44 20 7036 0660

SOUTH

✿ 40 MALTBY STREET
40 Maltby Street SE1 3PA
Tube / *Métro* : London Bridge (Northern/Jubilee)
+ 44 20 7237 9247

✿ ANGLESEA ARMS
15 Selwood Terrace, South Kensington, SW7 3QG
Tube / *Métro* : South Kensington (District/Circle/Piccadilly)
+ 44 20 7373 7960

✿ THE BOTANIST
No.7 Sloane Square SW1W 8EE
Tube / *Métro* : Sloane Square (District/Circle)
+ 44 20 7730 0077

✿ BISTRO UNION
40 Abbeville Road, Clapham, SW4 9NG
Tube / *Métro* : Clapham South (Northern)
+ 44 20 7042 6400

✿ CHEYNE WALK BRASSERIE
50 Cheyne Walk Chelsea SW3 5LR
Tube / *Métro* : Fulham Broadway (District)
+ 44 20 7376 8787

✿ THE CUT
Young Vic 66 The Cut SE1 8LZ UK
Tube / *Métro* : Waterloo (Bakerloo/Jubilee/Northern)
+ 44 20 7928 4400

🌹 THE DAIRY
15 The Pavement, Clapham Oldtown SW4 0HY
Tube / *Métro* : Clapham Common (Northern)
+ 44 20 7622 4165

🌹 THE DEAN SWIFT
10 Gainsford St, Butler's Wharf, London, SE1 2NE
Tube / *Métro* : Bermondsey (Jubilee)
+ 44 20 7357 0748

🌹 THE SHIP
41 Jew's Row, Wandsworth SW18 1TB
Tube / *Métro* : Wandsworth Town (Rail)
+ 44 20 8870 9667

🌹 THE GARRISON
99-101 Bermondsey St SE1 3XB
Tube / *Métro* : Borough (Northern)
+ 44 20 7089 9355

🌹 THE ORANGE
37 Pimlico Road SW1W 8NE
Tube / *Métro* : Sloane Square (Circle/District)
+ 44 20 7881 9844

🌹 PITT CUE
1 Newburgh St, Soho W1F 7RB
Tube / *Métro* : Oxford Circus (Bakerloo/Central/Victoria)
020 7287 5578

🌹 THE STAR TAVERN
6 Belgrave Mews West Belgravia SW1X 8HT
Tube / *Métro* : Knightsbridge (Piccadilly)
+ 44 20 7235 3019

EAST

☕ BUEN AYRE
☕ 50 Broadway Market E8 4QY
☕ Tube / *Métro* : London Fields (Overground)
   + 44 20 7275 9900

☕ THE GRAPES
☕ 76 Narrow Street E14 8BP
   Tube / *Métro* : Wetferry (DLR)
   + 44 20 7987 4396

☕ CHISWELL ST BAR & DINING ROOM
☕ No 56 Chiswell Street, EC1Y 4SA
☕ Tube / *Métro* : Barbican (Circle/Metropolitan)
   + 44 20 7614 0177

☕ THE CLOVE CLUB
☕ Shoreditch Town Hall 380 Old Street, London EC1V 9LT
☕ Tube / *Métro* : Old Street (Northern)
   + 44 20 7729 6496

☕ FOXLOW
☕ 71-73 Church Street, Stoke Newington N16 0AS
☕ Tube / *Métro* : Stoke Newington (Overground)
   + 44 20 7481 6377

☕ THE HAT AND TUN
☕ 3 Hatton Wall EC1N 8HX
   Tube / *Métro* : Farringdon (Circle/Metropolitan)
   + 44 20 7242 4747

THE HACK & HOP
35 Whitefriars Street EC4Y 8BH
Tube / *Métro* : Blackfriars (Circle/District)
+ 44 20 7583 8117

HAWKSMOOR SPITALFIELDS
157a Commercial Street, London E1 6BJ
Tube / *Métro* : Shoreditch High Street (Overground)
+ 44 20 7426 4850

THE MODERN PANTRY
47-48 St John's Square Clerkenwell EC1V 4JJ
Tube / *Métro* : Farringdon (Circle/Metropolitan)
+ 44 20 7553 9210

OLD RED COW
71/72 Long Lane, Barbican EC1A 9EJ
Tube / *Métro* : Barbican (Circle/Metropolitan)
+ 44 20 7726 2595

ONE CANADA SQUARE
1 Canada Square, Canary Wharf E14 5AB
Tube / *Métro* : Canary Wharf (DLR)
+ 44 20 7559 5199

THE OWL & PUSSYCAT
34 Redchurch Street E2 7DP
Tube / *Métro* : Shoreditch High Street (Overground)
+ 44 20 3487 0088

THE WELL
180 St John Street, Clerkenwell EC1V 4JY
Tube / *Métro* : Farringdon (Circle/Metropolitan)
+ 44 20 7251 9363

THE WHITE SWAN
108 Fetter Lane, EC4A 1ES
Tube / *Métro* : Chancery Lane (Central)
+ 44 20 7242 9696

THE WILMINGTON
69 Rosebery Avenue, Clerkenwell, EC1R 4RL
Tube / *Métro* : Farringdon (Circle/Metropolitan)
+ 44 20 7837 1384

ADRESSES CLASSÉES PAR ORDRE ALPHABÉTIQUE / *ADDRESSES LISTED IN ALPHABETICAL ORDER*

· ·

Par ordre alphabétique / *In alphabetical order*

PARIS

LONDRES / *LONDON*

PARIS – LONDON

SAS Éditions Lebey

Éditeur
Gérald de Roquemaurel

Président
Pierre-Yves Chupin

4, square de l'Alboni
75016 Paris
contact@lebey.com

Enquêteurs / *Food critics*
John Porter (researcher and writer London)

Yann Aledo, NT Binh, Laurent Berard-Quelin, Jérôme Bourret,
Antoine Buéno, Hughes Cazenave, Dominique Couvreur, Jonathan Dayot,
Rémi Dechambre, Gilles Dupuis, Marc Horwitz, Chantal Janisson,
Maxime Landemaine, Laura Lourdas, Sakiko Leblanc, Jacques Morel,
Guiral de Raffin, Jonathan Siksou, Philippe Toinard

Direction artistique / *Artistic direction*
Thomas Dossou

Traduction / *Translation*
Nicole Seeman

Publicité / *Advertising*
APM EVENTS
Pauline Juillard +33 (0)6 79 39 05 50

Diffusion exclusive UK / *Exclusive UK distribution*
Librairie La Page
www.librairielapage.com

Relations presse / *Press relations*
Brigitte de Roquemaurel

Choisi par
La Tour d'Argent

CUVÉE ROSÉ
INIMITABLE

CHAMPAGNE

Laurent-Perrier

MAISON FONDÉE
1812

Photographe : Iris Velghe / Illustration : Pierre Le Tan

Les découpes
d'agneau

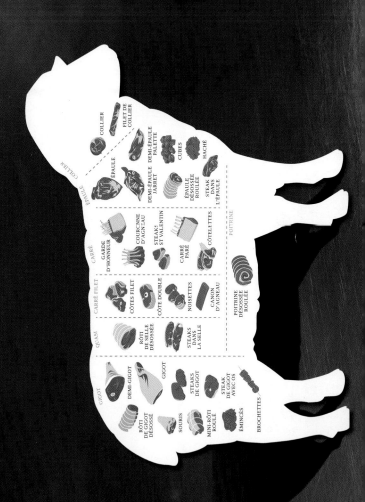

COLLIER

FILET DE COLLIER

COLLIER

ÉPAULE

ÉPAULE

DEMI-ÉPAULE PALETTE

CUBES

HACHÉ

DEMI-ÉPAULE JARRET

ÉPAULE DÉSOSSÉE ROULÉE

STEAK DANS L'ÉPAULE

CARRÉ

GARDE D'HONNEUR

COURONNE D'AGNEAU

STEAKS ST VALENTIN

CÔTELETTES

POITRINE

CARRÉ PARÉ

CARRÉ FILET

CÔTES FILET

CÔTE DOUBLE

NOISETTES

CANON D'AGNEAU

POITRINE DÉSOSSÉE ROULÉE

QUASI

RÔTI DE SELLE DÉSOSSÉE

STEAKS DANS LA SELLE

GIGOT

DEMI-GIGOT

GIGOT

STEAKS DE GIGOT

STEAK DE GIGOT AVEC OS

RÔTI DE GIGOT DÉSOSSÉ

SOURIS

MINI-RÔTI ROULÉ

ÉMINCÉS

BROCHETTES

NORME QUALITÉ
agneau
Britannique